SAVING
CHILDREN FROM THE
HOLOCAUST

The Kindertransport

Titles in
The Holocaust Through Primary Sources
Series:

AUSCHWITZ
Voices From the Death Camp
Library Ed. ISBN: 978-0-7660-3322-1
Paperback ISBN: 978-1-59845-346-1

KRISTALLNACHT
The Nazi Terror That Began the Holocaust
Library Ed. ISBN: 978-0-7660-3324-5
Paperback ISBN: 978-1-59845-345-4

LIBERATION
Stories of Survival From the Holocaust
Library Ed. ISBN: 978-0-7660-3319-1
Paperback ISBN: 978-1-59845-348-5

RESCUING THE DANISH JEWS
A Heroic Story From the Holocaust
Library Ed. ISBN: 978-0-7660-3321-4
Paperback ISBN: 978-1-59845-343-0

SAVING CHILDREN FROM THE HOLOCAUST
The Kindertransport
Library Ed. ISBN: 978-0-7660-3323-8
Paperback ISBN: 978-1-59845-344-7

THE WARSAW GHETTO UPRISING
Striking a Blow Against the Nazis
Library Ed. ISBN: 978-0-7660-3320-7
Paperback ISBN: 978-1-59845-347-8

SAVING
CHILDREN FROM THE
HOLOCAUST

The Kindertransport

The Holocaust Through Primary Sources

Ann Byers

Enslow Publishers, Inc.
40 Industrial Road
Box 398
Berkeley Heights, NJ 07922
USA
http://www.enslow.com

Library of Congress Cataloging-in-Publication Data

Byers, Ann.
      Saving children from the Holocaust : the Kindertransport / Ann Byers.
         p. cm. — (The Holocaust through primary sources)
      Summary: "Discusses the Kindertransport, including the people who organized the operation, how the transports worked, the children's lives who escaped on a transport, and how ten thousand children were saved from the Holocaust"—Provided by publisher.
       Includes bibliographical references and index.
       ISBN 978-0-7660-3323-8
       1. World War, 1939–1945—Jews—Rescue—Great Britain—Juvenile literature.
2. Kindertransports (Rescue operations)—Juvenile literature. 3. Jewish children in the Holocaust—Juvenile literature. 4. World War, 1939–1945—Biography—Juvenile literature. 5. Jews—Europe—Biography—Juvenile literature. 6. Righteous Gentiles in the Holocaust—Biography—Juvenile literature. 7. Jewish children—Europe—Biography—Juvenile literature. 8. Holocaust, Jewish (1939–1945)—Biography—Juvenile literature.
I. Title.
       DS135.E5B94 2011
       940.53'1835083—dc22   2010014215

Paperback ISBN 978-1-59845-344-7

Printed in China
052011 Leo Paper Group, Heshan City, Guangdong, China
10 9 8 7 6 5 4 3 2 1

To Our Readers: We have done our best to make sure all Internet addresses in this book were active and appropriate when we went to press. However, the author and the publisher have no control over and assume no liability for the material available on those Internet sites or on other Web sites they may link to. Any comments or suggestions can be sent by e-mail to comments@enslow.com or to the address on the back cover.

Every effort has been made to locate all copyright holders of material used in this book. If any errors or omissions have occurred, please contact us at www.enslow.com. We will try to make corrections in future editions.

Illustration Credits: Associated Press, pp. 28, 42, 48, 66, 71, 76, 88, 102, 108, 111, 112; Enslow Publishers, Inc., pp. 17, 46; The Granger Collection, New York, p. 86; Hulton Archive / Getty Images, p. 104; © Mary Evans / Heinz Zinram / The Image Works, p. 99; NYPL / Stephen A. Schwarzman Building / George Arents Collection, p. 96; Sueddeutsche Zeitung Photo / The Image Works, p. 74; USHMM, courtesy of Alfred Traum, p. 19; USHMM, courtesy of Anita Willens, p. 79; USHMM, courtesy of Bea Siegel Green, p. 35; USHMM, courtesy of Eva Rosenbaum Abraham-Podietz, p. 57; USHMM, courtesy of Frances Rose, p. 106; USHMM, courtesy of George Landecker, p. 91; USHMM, courtesy of Guenther Cahn, p. 95; USHMM, courtesy of Hans Levy, p. 38; USHMM, courtesy of Henry Schmelzer, p. 53; USHMM, courtesy of Herbert and Ursel Goldschmidt, p. 78; USHMM, courtesy of Inge Engelhard Sadan, pp. 61, 63, 69; USHMM, courtesy of Instytut Pamieci Narodowej, p. 22; USHMM, courtesy of Jacob G. Wiener, p. 81; USHMM, courtesy of Kurt Fuchel, p. 50; USHMM, courtesy of Lily Haber, p. 84; USHMM, courtesy of Lydia Chagoll, p. 34; USHMM, courtesy of Margot Stern Loewenberg, p. 31; USHMM, courtesy of Martin Smith, p. 11; USHMM, courtesy of Mimi Ormond, p. 44; USHMM, courtesy of National Archives and Records Administration, pp. 8, 12; USHMM, courtesy of Norbert Wollheim, p. 16; USHMM, courtesy of Trudy Isenberg, p. 10; USHMM, Wide World Photo, p. 55; USHMM, courtesy of Yad Vashem, p. 24.

Cover Illustration: USHMM, courtesy of Instytut Pamieci Narodowej (Jewish refugee children arrive in Harwich England on the first Kindertransport from Germany, December 2, 1938); USHMM, courtesy of Fritz Gluckstein (Star of David artifact).

Contents

Number 152

She tried to look at it as an adventure. It would be, after all, another country she could add to her collection. Lore Groszmann was keeping track of all the places she had been in her ten years. She called it "collecting countries." Austria was her home, and she had visited Hungary and Czechoslovakia. England would be number four.

This adventure, however, would be very different. This time, she would be going alone. Not exactly alone—six hundred other children would be going with her. But she did not know any of them. She had loving parents, grandparents, aunts, uncles, and cousins. But none of them would be coming with her.

Lore's Aunt Trude and Uncle Hans had already moved to England. They had left shortly after the *Anschluss* nine months earlier. On March 12, 1938, Adolf Hitler, the chancellor of Germany, had taken over Austria in a move called the *Anschluss*, uniting the two countries. He stationed troops in Austrian cities. In fact, German soldiers had set up one of their operations in Lore's grandparents' yard. Trude and Hans had left before the worst of Hitler's changes came to Austria.

Lore had felt many of those changes. She was Jewish, and Hitler hated Jews. His political party, the Nazi Party, was violently antisemitic—prejudiced against Jews. The antisemitic laws and practices that Hitler had begun in Germany were becoming part of life in Austria. Lore had to leave her school and go to a school for Jews only. Her Uncle Paul had been expelled from the University of Vienna because Jews were no longer permitted there. Lore's father lost his job, and her grandparents had their business taken from them. But through those changes, she was not alone.

Lore Groszmann witnessed Germany's takeover of Austria and the antisemitic laws the Nazis put in place. In this photo, Austrian Nazis and local residents look on as Jews are forced to scrub and clean the pavement of a street in Vienna.

Even on *Kristallnacht*, the Night of Broken Glass, her parents were there to comfort her. On the evening of November 9, vicious mobs attacked Jewish businesses, synagogues, and homes throughout Germany and Austria. At age ten, Lore was frightened:

> The wife of the elderly neighbor sat on a chair crying, in a thin voice, without intermission. The Nazis . . . kept turning the lights off, sometimes for as long as half an hour, then off and on, and off and on. Into the middle of this walked Tante [Aunt] Gusti's brother, hoping to hide out because his own apartment was being raided, but he was intercepted by the guard at the entrance and taken away. Tante Gusti stood in the doorway and wept. . . . I sat down and howled for my mother.[1]

But in that madness, at least Lore had her mother and father. Today, she would have no one.

Her father had tried to keep them all together. He knew they were not safe in Austria. He had made the rounds of all the foreign embassies in Vienna, seeking permission to go to another country—any other country. America, England, France, Panama, China, Switzerland—Lore's father put his family's name on every list. But it was of no use.

Residents in Ober Ramstadt, Germany, watch as the town's synagogue is burned to the ground. The German fire department is preventing the fire from spreading to other buildings but allows the synagogue to burn.

Representatives of thirty-two countries had held a conference in Evian, France, the previous July. They had talked about the hardships of the Jews in Nazi countries. Jews were trying to leave Germany and Austria. But the Nazis would not let them take any of their money with them, and no country wanted to accept penniless refugees.

There was one exception. Less than two weeks after Kristallnacht, Great Britain said it would receive some who were fleeing Nazi oppression. The offer was only temporary and only for those under the age of seventeen. They would be safe in England and would return home when the persecution ended. The project was called the *Kindertransport* (*Kinder* is German for "children"). If Lore's father could not get his entire family out of Austria, he could save at least his only child. He registered his daughter for one of the Kindertransports.

That is how Lore happened to be alone on the night of December 10, 1938. She was at the train station outside Vienna:

Evian, France, is shown in this postcard in 1938. Representatives from thirty-two countries held a meeting in the town to discuss the plight of the Jews in Nazi-controlled territory.

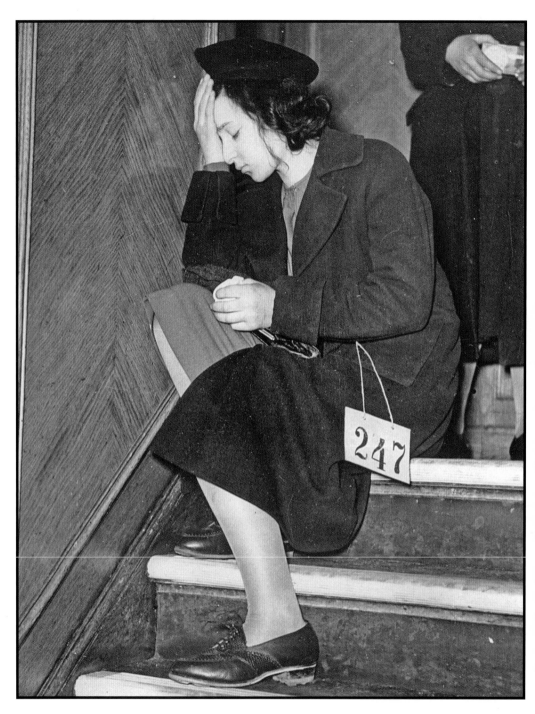

A young Jewish girl rests on a staircase shortly after her arrival in Harwich, England, on December 12, 1938. Her number, 247, on a tag hanging from her waist, identifies her as a child from a Kindertransport.

> *There was a confusion of kissing parents—*
> *my father bending down, my mother's face*
> *burning against mine. Before I could get a*
> *proper grip on my suitcase, the line set in*
> *motion so that the suitcase kept slipping from*
> *my hand and bumping against my legs. Panic-*
> *stricken, I looked to the right, but my mother*
> *was there, walking beside me. . . . "Go on,*
> *move," the children behind me said. We were*
> *passing through . . . doors. I looked to my right;*
> *my mother's face was nowhere to be seen.*[2]

Alone in the midst of hundreds of other frightened children, Lore carried, or rather dragged, her one small but heavy suitcase through the doors of the station. On her back was a rucksack (backpack), lovingly stuffed with bread, sausage, and candies. These were the only items she was allowed to bring aboard the train. A cardboard label around her neck and tags on her suitcase and rucksack identified her as *Kind* (child) number 152.[3]

Lore was one of nearly ten thousand children who made the trip from Nazi Europe to Great Britain. Nine months after the first train left, World War II began, and the transports stopped. The children stayed in England six long years as the war raged. A few lucky ones were reunited with their parents. Most lost their families in the Holocaust, Hitler's attempt to murder all the Jews of Europe.

Lore, of course, could not know any of that on that cold December night. All she knew was that she was embarking on an adventure . . . and she was going alone.

The German Idealist: Norbert Wollheim

Norbert Wollheim, born and raised in Berlin, did not feel persecuted in Germany. His family was assimilated, which means his parents did not separate themselves from the rest of the population. They worked and lived like any other German. He recalled: "I was in a non-Jewish high school. We had not too many Jewish children. I met a certain amount of anti-Semitism, but not militant anti-Semitism, but what we called more a kind of cultural anti-Semitism. But we managed."[1]

As soon as he was old enough, at age thirteen, Norbert joined the Jewish Youth Movement. The movement consisted of groups that instilled Jewish values and pride in young Jews. Members studied Jewish writers, sang inspirational songs, and enjoyed social activities, such as hiking. One of the strongest teachings of the movement was the importance of helping others. Wollheim said, "We all hoped to create a new and better world, and we tried to contribute to that by doing social work."[2] After high school, in 1931, Wollheim enrolled in the University of Berlin. He planned to help create a new and better world by becoming a lawyer.

Changes in Germany

But in less than two years, his dream was shattered. Hitler became chancellor of Germany, and he outlawed Jews from practicing law.

Wollheim was now less concerned with changing the world than with leaving the country. He had a plan:

In 1935 I joined a firm, a Jewish firm, a reputable firm in the import-export business specializing in metal trade and ore trade. This firm had excellent business contacts with England, Sweden, France, and the eastern countries, so it was my hope that when I would join that firm, I could establish also some kind of a contact in order to find a way out.[3]

That job lasted barely three years. In September 1938, the company, like all others throughout Germany, was taken away from its Jewish owner and given to an "Aryan," what the Nazis called their idealized, pure-blooded German race. All the Jewish workers were fired. Wollheim had to find another way to leave Germany:

I came to the conclusion that I should try my best to try to get out. I got married in 1938, in summer of 1938. Things in Berlin were not pleasant. . . . We all tried then strongly to get out. We registered under the quota system at the American consulate, for instance. And I felt a responsibility also to do something for my parents.[4]

Because he had no job, Wollheim took advantage of some vocational training offered by a Jewish organization. He learned welding, figuring it was a trade he could use anywhere. And he wrote to his contacts abroad. In a U.S. telephone book, he found a family in Chicago with the last name Wollheim. In his desperation, he wrote, asking the Chicago Wollheims if they would sponsor their "relatives" to come to America. Amazingly, they responded . . . but not in time.

Norbert Wollheim sits on a ship deck while accompanying German-Jewish children to a summer camp in Horserod, Denmark. Before his work on the Kindertransport, Wollheim was active in Jewish organizations in Germany.

KRISTALLNACHT

After Hitler became chancellor of Germany, the persecution of Jews in Nazi Germany became increasingly harsh. It began with a nationwide boycott of Jewish businesses. Then antisemitism was legalized in the Nuremberg laws. These laws stripped Jews of their economic, social, and human rights. The persecution continued with Hitler's order that all Jews in Germany who had been born in Poland be sent back across the border.

In October 1938, the Nazi Gestapo loaded seventeen thousand Jews into railroad cars and drove them to Poland. But the Polish government would not let them in. The Gestapo abandoned them at the border, where they remained for several days without food or shelter. One of the Poles sent a postcard to his son, Herschel Grynszpan, describing the family's terrible ordeal.

Grynszpan was in Paris, a seventeen-year-old student. Enraged, he went to the German embassy with a gun. He wanted to take out his anger on some German official. When he saw Ernst vom Rath, a secretary, he thought he was Germany's ambassador to France, and he shot him.

The Nazis used this assassination as an excuse for widespread violence against Jews. On the night of November 9, men of various Nazi police forces descended on Jewish businesses, synagogues, and homes all over Germany and Austria. They carried clubs, axes, and bombs. Dressed as civilians, they broke windows, looted shops, and burned buildings. They dragged Jews from their homes, beat them, and destroyed their property. The uniformed police merely watched.

The rampage became known as Kristallnacht—the Night of Broken Glass. The Nazis called it a "spontaneous reaction" to vom Rath's death, but it was obviously a well-organized attack. When it was over, 7,500 shops had been destroyed, 267 synagogues and 171 homes burned, and at least 91 people killed. Thirty thousand Jews were arrested and sent to concentration camps. The Jewish community was then required to pay a fine of one billion marks (equal to $400 million). Kristallnacht marked the beginning of undisguised violence against the Jews of Germany and Austria.

During the terror of Kristallnacht, Jewish homes and shops were destroyed, and many Jews were murdered. This map shows the cities and towns across Germany and Austria where synagogues were burned down.

After Kristallnacht, Wollheim volunteered in the relief agencies of the Jewish community in Berlin. He helped organize the delivery of food, clothing, medical attention, transportation, and other help to those who needed it most.

The Children's Transports

At the same time, Otto Hirsch, director of the German Jewish Federation, learned of England's offer to provide shelter for ten thousand of Germany's Jewish children. Hirsch just had to figure out how to get them there. Who could he put in charge of such a massive undertaking? Hirsch thought of twenty-five-year-old Wollheim. He had put programs together. He had organized relief efforts. He had even taken children on trains before. He approached Wollheim for his help: "He called me and said . . . 'We have terrific social workers . . . but they need technical help and this is something you have to do.'"[5]

At first, Wollheim hesitated. It was a larger operation than he had ever tackled. Besides, he was trying to get his family out of the country. Hirsch assured him that after the children were safe, Hirsch would help Wollheim and his family emigrate. True to the principles he had always lived by, Wollheim said yes.

The task was even greater than Wollheim expected. First, children had to be identified. They had to be under the age of seventeen. The ones in the greatest danger should go to England first—those who had been in concentration camps and would be imprisoned again if caught. The ones whose fathers were still in the camps. The children with no parents. They had to pass a health inspection. England did not want the additional burden of caring for sick children.

Jewish communities throughout Germany gathered names and documents of children. They sent the papers to Wollheim in Berlin. Wollheim secured trains in Germany and Holland and ferries from Holland to England. He decided which children would go on which transport. He sent lists of their names to the authorities in England. The Gestapo, the Nazi police, needed lists, too, and Wollheim made sure they were in order.

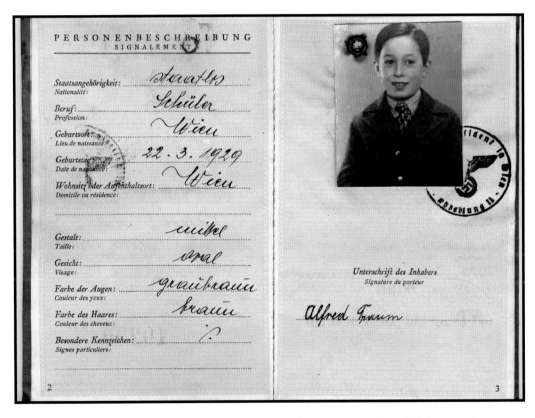

Norbert Wollheim collected documents and passports for children going on the Kindertransports. This passport was issued to Alfred Traum prior to his departure from Vienna, Austria, on a Kindertransport.

Coordinating all the details across three countries required much time on the telephone. Communication lines were not good, so a single call could take three or four hours. Wollheim and many other social workers labored night and day scheduling the trains and contacting parents to tell them when and where to meet.

Then came the most difficult part: watching parents leave their children. The Gestapo would not allow the parting to take place in public. They did not want other Germans riding the trains to witness emotional scenes. So Wollheim rented a room large enough to hold the children, their parents, and their brothers and sisters who were not going. The young man stood on a chair and gave them instructions:

"Ladies and gentlemen, the time has arrived to say goodbye, because we are under strict orders not to let you accompany your children to the platform. The escorts will take over . . . you cannot come. . . . Please cooperate and don't make our work more difficult. But this is the time you have to say good-bye."

There were last kisses and last hugs. . . . But in general I still admire these people, how courageous they were. Nobody broke down, but also there was the expectation that sooner or later they would be reunited again.[6]

Years later, Wollheim wondered how he had the courage to make such a speech to frightened and grieving parents. His short answer:

At this time we didn't know and we couldn't even foresee, we couldn't surmise for a moment that for many or most, it would be the last goodbye, that most of those children would never see their parents again.[7]

Riding the Trains

One of Wollheim's more difficult tasks was finding people who would ride with the children. Only a few escorts were allowed. At first, they could ride only as far as the border; they could not leave Germany. After the first few transports, the Gestapo agreed to let the escorts go all the way to England, but they had to come back right away. If they did not, the whole operation would stop. Wollheim was extremely careful in choosing escorts.

He rode on the first transport. He needed to see what would happen once the train left the station. Whatever problems he encountered, he might be able to fix on the next transport. The first Kindertransport left Berlin on December 1, 1938. It carried 196 children, all from an orphanage destroyed on Kristallnacht. When it reached the place where it was to cross into Holland, it stopped. Wollheim expected customs officials to come on board to inspect documents. He had everything in order. But it was not courteous customs officials who performed the inspection; it was callous SS guards. They were not interested in the passengers' papers, but in their belongings. They thought the children might be carrying expensive items with them. Like savage animals, they pawed through the small suitcases of the frightened children. Wollheim could do nothing to stop them.

Norbert Wollheim accompanied the children on the trains on the first Kindertransport when it left Berlin on December 1, 1938. These young children rest on a couch in Harwich, England, after arriving on the first Kindertransport.

In all, Wollheim organized about twenty transports to England from Berlin, Hamburg, Munich, and Frankfurt. He arranged a few others that took children to Sweden. He estimated that six thousand to seven thousand children were taken to safety on those trains.[8]

Deported

Almost nine months after the first Kindertransport left Berlin, in late August 1939, Wollheim considered escorting another train. But his wife was pregnant, and he did not want to leave her. That transport turned out to be the last one to depart from Germany; war broke out days later. Barely a year afterward, Otto Hirsch was arrested and killed in a concentration camp, so he could not make good on his promise to help Wollheim and his family escape.

Wollheim went back to working with young people in the shrinking Jewish community in Berlin. The only hope for Jews, who could not attend school or hold jobs, was to learn a trade. If they could ever get out of Germany, they would need some way of earning a living in a new country. Wollheim was a fair welder, so he taught welding to young Jewish boys.

But the Nazis were in the process of "cleansing" Germany of anything and everyone Jewish. In December 1942, Wollheim's parents were deported from Berlin to Auschwitz, a Nazi death camp. His turn came the following spring. Once more he rode a train. This one, however, was a cattle car—without seats, lights, or toilets. It went directly to Auschwitz.

When Norbert Wollheim was taken to Auschwitz, his wife and young son were sent to the gas chambers. Wollheim was selected for forced labor. Pictured here, these men at Auschwitz-Birkenau await further processing after being selected for forced labor.

At the death camp, Wollheim's pregnant wife and three-year-old son were sent immediately to the gas chamber. Wollheim was taken, along with other men, to the Buna/Monowitz subcamp. The number 107984 was tattooed on his arm. He was part of the unnamed slave labor force of the camp, working in the synthetic rubber factory of I. G. Farben. It was brutal:

[The camp] was a vast area of mud. . . . To walk was very difficult, took a lot of strength. . . . For newcomers, this was the destiny, you were destined to do the most difficult work, which was transport and digging, and this was not just done in a leisurely way, but mostly running around with cement and iron and things like that. . . . When the rain came down, and these bags, these cement bags opened, then cement turned into cake and it covered your clothing and your body, and . . . there was hardly any chance to keep clean because we were not allowed to possess anything. . . . Without being able to keep clean, all kind of disasters could strike, diseases and so on. . . . You come back to a very, very primitive kind of existence.[9]

Because he was a welder, Wollheim was eventually transferred to an inside work detail, out of the summer heat and the winter cold. This, he said later, saved his life. For two long and grueling years, Wollheim toiled at the camp.

When the war ended and he was freed, he learned that he was the only one of seventy relatives to survive. He returned to Germany and his life's work of helping others. In the city of Lubeck, he helped rebuild the Jewish community and Jewish pride. In 1952, with his new wife and two children, he immigrated to the United States, where he became an accountant. He remained active in promoting understanding and justice until his death in 1998 at age eighty-five.

The Dutch Aunt:
Gertrud Wijsmuller-Meijer

The violent assault against the Jews on Kristallnacht sparked outrage around the world. In England, members of groups trying to help Jews flee Nazi Germany met with British government leaders. England, like nearly every other country, had closed its doors to refugees. Opening them could bring a flood that Britain said it could not afford. The groups had an idea. Perhaps they could rescue at least the children. The children could stay in England until the ugliness in Germany was over. The operation would not cost the government anything. The groups would raise the money from private citizens. They would find people who would take the children into their homes and pay for their care.

The groups, which evolved into the Refugee Children's Movement, presented their plan. Home secretary Sir Samuel Hoare explained their reasoning to Parliament: "Here is a chance of taking in the young generation of a great people, of mitigating [lessening] to some extent the terrible sufferings of their parents."[1]

After some discussion, others agreed. England would admit children up to the age of seventeen. Before they could come, each child needed a sponsor. They could stay only for a time. They would eventually have to either go back to their homes or to some other country. To cover that cost, the refugee organization had to deposit 50 pounds (British currency, equivalent to about $3,060 today) for each child. And the refugee organization would need to pay for the cost of the entire operation.

There was no time to lose. Lord Stanley Baldwin, a former prime minister, made a public plea for funds. In a radio broadcast, he appealed to people's consciences and their hearts:

> Thousands of men, women, and children, despoiled of their goods, driven from their homes, are seeking asylum and sanctuary on our doorsteps, a hiding place from the wind and a cover from the tempest. They may not be our fellow subjects, but they are our fellow men. Tonight I plead for the victims who turn to England for help. . . . The honour of our country is challenged, our Christian charity is challenged, and it [is] up to us to meet that challenge.[2]

The speech was effective. In six months, people donated 500,000 pounds. They also signed up as sponsors. Some offered their houses and farms. A department store gave shoes. Much of England rose to meet Lord Baldwin's challenge. The next hurdle was on the other end, in Germany and Austria. Who would select the children and get the parents to agree to let them go?

Lord Stanley Baldwin in a radio broadcast made a public request for funds to assist in the effort of saving children from Nazi Germany.

Who would obtain permissions from the Nazi government for the children to leave? Who would arrange for the buses, trains, and boats to England? To find the right people, the Refugee Children's Movement sent representatives to Germany, Austria, and the countries along the route.

Dutch Connection

One of the most helpful people was a woman in the Netherlands. Gertrud Wijsmuller-Meijer, born into a prosperous shipping family and married to a wealthy banker, spoke German fluently. As the only girl among five brothers, she learned early to be very tough.

She was used to getting what she wanted, and she was not afraid of anyone or anything.

However, her gruffness was outmatched by her kindness and generosity. She spent her time and her money helping others. Although she had no children of her own, she loved children dearly. Many knew her as Aunt Truus. Long before anyone from England contacted her, she, a Christian woman, worked with the Dutch Committee for Jewish Affairs. She organized shipments of food and medicine to needy people throughout Europe.

The representatives from England asked the German-speaking Dutch woman to go to Austria. That was where the Office for

THE NETHERLANDS AND THE HOLOCAUST

The name "Netherlands" means "low lands" or "low countries." The country originally made up part of the southern, or lower, territories of the Hapsburg empire of the sixteenth century. It is often called "Holland" after two of its provinces. Its people and language are Dutch.

When Germany started World War II, the Netherlands declared itself neutral. The Dutch would not take sides, and they would not fight. But Hitler violated that neutrality. On May 10, 1940, Germany invaded the Netherlands.

Almost immediately, the Nazi government of the occupied country began to persecute the Dutch Jews. Almost 160,000 Jews lived in the Netherlands; 25,000 of them had fled from the same oppression in Germany and Austria.

The people of the Netherlands, by and large, were not antisemitic. When hundreds of Jews were arrested and sent to the Buchenwald and Mauthausen concentration camps in Germany, non-Jewish workers in Dutch factories went on strike.

The Nazis responded by cracking down even harder. They separated the Jews from other Dutch people, forcing them to wear the yellow Star of David on their clothing. They imprisoned Dutch Jews in forced labor camps and foreign Jews in transit camps, awaiting transport to the death camps of Poland.

The meticulous records the Nazis kept show that 107,000 Jews were deported from the Netherlands. Of those, only 5,200 survived.

Jewish Emigration was located, headed by Adolf Eichmann. Eichmann's job was to get all the Jews in Germany and Austria to leave and to squeeze all their money out of them before they left.

Confronting Eichmann

Wijsmuller-Meijer was not intimidated by Eichmann, one of the most ruthless of all Nazi officials. Years later, she recalled details of her encounter:

> *He sat in a large room. You come into it from the front, and Dr. Eichmann sat at the other end in a black uniform, with a large lamp and a huge dog. I went to him and said: "Doctor, I'm Mrs. Wijsmuller and would like to talk to you." But he told me with strict voice that he was not accustomed to women to speak, and that I should go.[3]*

Unfazed by Eichmann's attempt to brush her off, Wijsmuller-Meijer apologized for not bringing her husband and plopped herself down in a chair.

Surprised by her boldness, Eichmann listened. She asked for written permission to take six hundred Jewish children out of Austria. She would arrange for the transportation. A boat would be waiting in Holland to take them to England.

Adolf Eichmann set severe restrictions for what children could bring on their journey to England. Only one suitcase was allowed per child. Margot Stern, who went to England on a Kindertransport, had this label on her suitcase.

Kindertransport

Nr.

2688

des Hilfsvereins der Juden in Deutschland e. V.
Berlin W 35, Ludendorffstr. 20

Eichmann was baffled. Sitting before him was an obviously "Aryan" woman—a tall, blonde, blue-eyed German who fit the Nazi ideal of the perfect race. And yet she wanted to care for Jewish children. He could only conclude that she was crazy. He would give her what she asked, but with strict requirements. If she could meet his demands, she could have the children.

The children could take only one suitcase and one bag each. No toys and no books. They could have no more money than 10 Reichsmarks. They could each take one photograph, but only one. Parents could not accompany them as far as the trains; he wanted no emotional displays. A few adults could ride in the trains with the children, but they had to come back. He would issue one mass exit visa, but all the children's names and information had to be recorded. She had four days.

The First Transport

The task was enormous, but Aunt Truus was up to the challenge. She scheduled and paid for the train. She made sure the steamboat *Prague* would be ready. She arranged for people in Holland to help transfer the refugees from the train to the boat. The Jewish community in Vienna had selected the children who would go and registered their names. On Saturday, December 10, 1938, the first children's transport from Austria left Vienna with six hundred on board.

It was the second Kindertransport. The first had gone from Berlin nine days earlier. These were experimental evacuations. England had not yet officially authorized the operation. Large sums of money had not yet been raised. But the members of the refugee organizations could not wait any longer. They were racing against time.

The train traveled north, through Germany. Lore Groszmann Segal remembered vividly what happened when it reached Holland:

> The train rode into a station and stopped. The big girl [an older Kind] said this was the border and now the Nazis would decide what to do with us. She told us to sit as quiet as we could. There was much walking about outside. We saw uniforms under the lights on the platform. They entered the train in front. I held myself so still that my head vibrated on

my neck and my knees cramped. Half an hour, an hour. . . . They were coming toward us down the corridor, stopping at each compartment door. Then one of them stood in our doorway. His uniform had many buttons. . . . The Nazi signed to one of the children to come with him, and she followed him out. . . . They were taking one child from each carriage to check papers and look for contraband [forbidden items].

When the little girl returned, she sat down in her place and we all stared at her. We did not ask her what had happened, and she never told us. The carriage rocked; the Nazis had got off. Doors slammed. The train moved. Someone shouted, "We're out!" Then everyone was pressing into the corridor. Everyone was shouting and laughing. I was laughing.[4]

Within minutes, the train pulled to a stop in Holland. Bright lights shone on throngs of people. Aunt Truus had arranged for this welcoming committee. Smiling Dutch people came to the train's windows with apples, sandwiches, chocolate, and cups of hot tea. One hundred children got off at this brief stop. The boat to England could hold only five hundred, and some would have to wait for the next transport. The rest continued to the Hook of Holland, a town in the southern part of the Netherlands. From there, Harwich, England, was six hours away.

A little girl sleeps with her doll in a chair after her arrival in England on December 12, 1938. She had left Vienna, Austria, on the second Kindertransport, one that Aunt Truus had helped organize.

Gutsy Lady

The train from Vienna was not the last for Wijsmuller-Meijer. In all, she organized forty-nine of the children's transports from Germany and Austria. Her courage and boldness proved crucial to their success.

On one occasion, she was waiting with other Dutch women at the border station in Holland. They were ready for the train from Berlin—with welcome treats and passage to the Hook. But when the train arrived, no Jewish children were aboard. Aunt Truus went to the Bentheim station across the border to see what had happened.

She discovered that at the German station, Nazi agents had been especially vicious in their inspection. They had ripped open the children's luggage, tearing into everything, even tubes of toothpaste. They hoped to find items of value. The fruitless search threatened to make

Three girls look out a train window as they leave Munich, Germany, in June 1939 on a Kindertransport to England.

the other passengers late. So the two cars of Jewish children had been uncoupled from the train.

When Wijsmuller-Meijer heard the story, she scolded the Nazis sharply. When she was through, the Germans sheepishly returned the children's belongings to them. They hooked the cars to the next train, and the children continued on their way to England.[5]

Another Kindertransport from Berlin was stopped in Cologne. The Germans, only days away from beginning a war, were not permitting trains to go into Holland. Manfred Alweiss, fourteen and frightened, described what happened:

> To our immense relief, two buses arrived from Holland [the] next morning, to drive us across the frontier and then to the Hook. We learned much later, that these buses had been organised by a courageous lady (a Gentile) from the Dutch refugee committee [Gertrud Wijsmuller-Meijer]. She personally took charge of us. When we reached the frontier we were confronted by a frontier guard who stood, somewhat dramatically, in the middle of the road, with his rifle raised as if he was about to fire at us. Our plucky lady protector got out and showed our transit papers to the guard. After some consultation, he waved us through. . . . I will never forget the immense feeling of relief which swept through the bus the moment we crossed the border.[6]

The Last Transport

The Kindertransports from Germany, Czechoslovakia, and
Austria stopped abruptly on September 1, 1939. That was the day
Hitler and the Nazis invaded Poland, beginning World War II.
However, Holland remained a safe haven for a few more months.
But the German army invaded Holland on May 10. Wijsmuller-
Meijer did not have much time to get the Jewish children who
remained in the Netherlands out of the country.

On May 14, she was at an orphanage in Amsterdam with five
buses. She put eighty refugee children on the buses and headed to
the harbor where a boat bound for England was anchored. The
roads to the sea were glutted with vehicles, bicycles, and people
fleeing the German tanks. She wormed her way to the dock and
managed to get her children aboard the *Bodegraven*, the last ship
to leave. At ten minutes to eight, she stood on the dock, waving
good-bye. At eight o'clock, Holland surrendered to Germany.
The *Bodegraven* was the last of the Kindertransports.

More Work to Do

When the ship sailed, the captain asked Aunt Truus to come
with them. She refused, saying she had more work to do. The
Kindertransports were not the only way to get Jews out of Nazi
clutches. She chartered planes and flew some children to Britain.
And England was not the only refuge for small groups. She
smuggled Jewish children and adults to Sweden, Switzerland,
Spain, and Palestine (present-day Israel).

Many of the Jews she could not rescue were placed in the Westerbork camp. This was a transit camp the Nazis had set up in the Netherlands. It held people until they could be shipped to the death camps. Wijsmuller-Meijer worked with relief organizations to keep a needed supply of food, clothing, and medicine flowing into the camp.

Near the end of the war, she visited Westerbork and learned that fifty orphaned children were to be deported to Auschwitz, the largest Nazi death camp. She could not let that happen.

A group portrait of Jewish children in the Netherlands, who had gone there on a Kindertransport. Shortly after this photo was taken, the group went to England on May 14, 1940, aboard the SS *Bodegraven*, the last ship to leave before the Netherlands surrendered to Germany.

She went to the man in charge with a completely ridiculous story. The children, she told him, were not Jewish. They were the children of German soldiers by Dutch girls. They were, therefore, Aryan. Surely, he would not send Aryan children to their deaths.

Whether the man believed her is not certain. What is known is that he did not send the orphans to Auschwitz. They were sent to a different camp, where the Nazis exchanged them for other prisoners.[7]

When the war ended and the need for rescue and relief was over, this gutsy lady continued to help others. She spent many years helping create jobs for people with severe disabilities. In 1980, two years after her death at age eighty-two, a foundation was established in her name for mentally handicapped children and adolescents.

The nation of Israel has an organization dedicated to documenting and remembering people and events of the Holocaust: Yad Vashem. It honors non-Jews who saved Jews at the risk of their own lives. It calls such people Righteous Gentiles. Among the many honors she has received, one is that Gertrud Wijsmuller-Meijer has the distinction of being named a Righteous Gentile.

The British Stockbroker: Nicholas Winton

While Jewish children in Germany and Austria were being whisked westward to England, Jews in western Czechoslovakia were fleeing east. Hitler had added a strip of northwestern Czechoslovakia to his territory in October 1938. The area, called the Sudetenland, was home to many Jews. Thousands fled the persecution they knew would come. In and around Prague, the capital, refugee camps sprang up almost overnight. The camps were cold, crowded, and miserable. They were not the sort of places most people would choose for their vacations. Yet that is exactly where Nicholas Winton, a clerk at the London Stock Exchange, was headed for Christmas.

Vacation in Prague

Winton had been planning to go to Switzerland. Every year, he and a friend took a group of schoolboys skiing over the Christmas break. In 1938, however, his friend asked Winton to cancel the Switzerland trip and join him in Prague. He did not explain why. Always up for adventure, Winton went.

What he found in Czechoslovakia stunned him. Hundreds of families were huddled in squalor and fear, refugees from Hitler's takeover of their country. Winton's friend was working with other English men and women from the British Committee for Refugees from Czechoslovakia. They were trying to get those on Hitler's "wanted" list out of the country and in to England. Winton was moved by the refugees' desperation:

> *The situation was heartbreaking. Many of the refugees hadn't the price of a meal. Some of the mothers tried desperately to get money to buy food for themselves and their children. The parents desperately wanted at least to get their children to safety when they couldn't manage to get visas for the whole family. I began to realize what suffering there is when armies start to march.[1]*

Winton also realized that the German army would march again. Hitler would not stop with the Sudetenland; he wanted all of Czechoslovakia. The refugees would not be safe in Prague for much longer. Winton later recalled:

> *I could see in England what the political situation was and I thought it was much more serious than the politicians did. . . . Although there was an organization which was trying to get out the elder people, they had no permission from the British Government and they had no financial means to get out the children. So I merely said, if it was possible, I would do it.[2]*

Thousands of Jews fled the Sudetenland region of Czechoslovakia after the Nazis annexed the territory in 1938. Refugee camps, like the one pictured here, were hastily set up around Prague, the capital city.

Organizing the Rescue

With no experience in anything but buying and selling stocks, twenty-nine-year-old Winton contacted the governments of all the countries he thought might receive the children, including the United States. Only Sweden and Great Britain agreed to let them in.

Winton quickly turned his hotel room into an office and began to sign up children. "And in fact it wasn't really difficult," he said later. "It was a lot of hard work, but it wasn't difficult. . . . The Germans were in Prague, and the Germans were only too willing to get rid of these children."[3] And the parents leaped at the chance to send their children to safety.

On January 12, 1939, Winton put twenty children on an airplane to Sweden. The Scandinavian countries eventually took about two hundred children. But that was not enough. Winton turned to England.

England imposed the same restrictions as it did on the Kindertransports from Germany and Austria. A deposit of 50 pounds was needed for each child. The government would not pay for the transportation; everything had to be done with private funds. And, Winton recalled, "I could only bring in a child if I had a family that would look after them."[4]

Winton returned home to raise the money and find the sponsors. His "vacation" was ending anyway. He left the task of registering children in Prague to two British workers, Trevor Chadwick and Bill Barazetti.

To ask people to support the children's cause, Winton thought he needed to appear official. He should be part of some rescue organization. The group he left in Prague was called the British Committee for Refugees from Czechoslovakia. He tacked the words "Children's Section" on that name and created an "official" committee. He appointed himself honorary secretary and enlisted his mother's help. By day, Winton worked in the Stock Exchange; by night and whenever else he could, he rescued children.

From Prague, Chadwick sent pictures of children waiting for sponsors. Winton placed the photos in newspapers, in churches, and in synagogues. He talked to everyone who would listen. Funds trickled in. People came forward to say that they would take children. Some were from Jewish congregations, some from

Mimi Schleissner (right), a Czech Jew born in the Sudetenland, escaped Nazi territory on a Kindertransport train organized by Nicholas Winton. This family portrait was taken in December 1938, only months before she left for England. Her brother, Edward (left), and parents also survived the war.

Quaker churches, and others from no organized group at all. The need was so great, Winton accepted nearly every sponsor who responded. He realized that every placement might not be ideal, but he was convinced the alternative was death.

The British government had to issue entry visas for the young refugees. Sometimes red tape slowed the process of printing the documents. "Officials at the Home Office worked very slowly with the entry visas," Winton remembered. "We went to them urgently asking for permits, only to be told languidly, 'Why rush, old boy? Nothing will happen in Europe.'"[5]

Winton knew better. He had been in Czechoslovakia and seen the panic and despair. He could not wait. When the official papers did not come quickly enough, he simply forged visas.

Within two months, all the pieces finally came together. Chadwick and Barazetti had the names of six thousand Czech children. They had exit visas permitting them to leave. Their group would get the children out of the country. Winton would bring the sponsors to Liverpool Street Station in London to meet the children.

The Transports

The first train to leave Prague for England departed on March 14, 1939. The next day, Germany invaded Czechoslovakia. Now Winton felt even greater urgency. Escape routes were closing. Nazis harassed the committee's people in Prague. Reports of Nazi cruelty were being heard more frequently. Winton immediately set up another escape. In the next five months, until August 2, he and his group arranged seven more transports. They went by train from Prague through Germany and the Netherlands, then by ferry to England. The eight transports carried 669 Czech children to safety.[6]

The biggest evacuation was scheduled for September 1. That was the day Germany invaded Poland, beginning World War II. Winton lamented:

Within hours of the announcement [of the invasion], the train disappeared. None of the 250 children aboard was seen again. We had 250 families waiting at Liverpool Street that day in vain. If the train had been a day earlier, it would have come through. Not a single one of those children was heard of again, which is an awful feeling.[7]

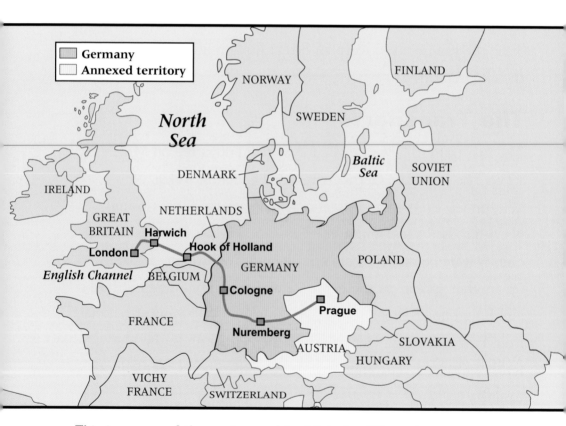

This is a map of the route used by Nicholas Winton's transports from Prague to London. Winton helped 669 Czech children reach safety on this route.

After the Transports

Once the war started, Winton's work in Czechoslovakia was over. There was no way to get any more people out of Nazi-occupied countries. Fifteen thousand Czech children perished in the Holocaust; Winton and his group saved nearly seven hundred. He could do no more.

But he could help in other places. He offered his services to the Red Cross. As part of an ambulance unit, he spent eight months in France, tending the wounded. Then he returned to England. When the war ended, he did not talk about what he had done. He married Grete, a Danish woman, and settled into a quiet life.

He would have been content in his silence for the rest of his days. But that was not to be. One day in 1988, nearly fifty years after he first went to Prague, Grete was in the attic of their home. She came across a leather briefcase she had not seen before. Inside was a scrapbook. It contained a long list of names and pictures of children. They were the photos Chadwick had sent, the ones that had appeared in newspapers so many years earlier. Grete found letters some parents had written to her husband. Winton had not even told his wife of his heroic deeds.

Grete, however, thought people should know. She shared her find with Elisabeth Maxwell, a historian of the Holocaust. Maxwell's husband was a wealthy newspaper publisher who had been born in Czechoslovakia. Between the two of them, they saw

Sir Nicholas Winton, age one hundred, smiles at a young relative at the Liverpool Street Station in London on September 4, 2009. Winton was attending a ceremony commemorating the seventieth anniversary of the Kindertransports that he helped organize in 1939.

that the story of this quiet man who helped save so many Czech children was printed in England's newspapers.

The newspaper articles led to an appearance on nationwide television. Some of the 669 Kinder who still lived in England, adults now, wept when they saw the program. Most of the children he rescued did not know of his role in their escape. Some thought the Red Cross had carried out the operation. Winton was flooded with calls, letters, and visits from grateful Kinder. They began to call themselves "Winton's children," and some dubbed Winton "the British Schindler" (after Oskar

Schindler, who saved twelve hundred Jews of Poland). Vera Gissing, one of Winton's children, said:

> *I owe him my life and those of my children and grandchildren. He rescued the greater part of the Jewish children of my generation in Czechoslovakia. Very few of us met our parents again—they perished in concentration camps. Had we not been spirited away, we would have been murdered alongside them.*[8]

After the story became public, Winton received many honors. At least two movies were made of his life and deeds. In 2002, he was knighted by Queen Elizabeth. Of all the thanks and praises, however, perhaps the one he treasures most is a ring presented to him by some of the Kinder. It is inscribed with words from the Jewish Talmud: "Save one life, save the world."

urt Fuchel had it good. His father, a manager of a bank, made enough money for Kurt's mother to stay home and dote on their only child. Their home in Vienna was large and beautiful. In addition to his parents and his grandmother, the nursemaid, Mitzi, tended to the boy's every need. Life was pleasant.

Kurt Fuchel's mother, Olga, stands for a photo with her dogs in their home in Vienna, Austria. The Nazis took the Fuchels' apartment after the Anschluss.

But the seven-year-old's world changed dramatically after the Anschluss. When Austria became part of Hitler's empire, Kurt could feel a different atmosphere in his home. He wrote:

> "Times are bad," Mutti [Mother] says. Papa doesn't go to work any more, and he doesn't talk much. He plays with me, but he doesn't smile. I ask, "What is the matter? Was I bad? Did I make too much noise?" . . . Papa tells me, "Times are bad, but it will pass."[1]

But it didn't pass; it got worse:

> I'm not allowed to go to my old school with my friends anymore! I have to take the tram all the way to the end and then walk through some woods. The school isn't a real school, but a house. . . . All the big people furniture is pushed up against the wall, and we sit on little stools in the middle of the room. There are only ten of us and we are all Jewish.[2]

A very social child, Kurt talked with the adults on the tram. He repeated what he had heard at home. And at home, the talk was about Hitler, about the terrible things he was doing to Austria. Somehow word got back to his parents that young Kurt spoke negatively about the country's new leader. From then on, his father rode the tram to school with him, and he was silent.

His father could come with him every day because he had lost his job. After the Anschluss, all the Jews in Vienna were fired from their work. To earn some money, Kurt's mother made and sold cloth flowers. They did not have to worry about paying Mitzi; she had to leave because Aryans were no longer allowed to work for Jews.

Another huge change came on Kristallnacht, eight months after the Anschluss. Their lovely apartment was taken away from them and given to a non-Jewish family. Like hundreds of other Jews throughout the city, they had to abandon most of their belongings and crowd into rooms with other families.

But the next change was the most drastic of all:

One day Papa tells me that we are going to move again, but not together. He and Mutti will put me on a train and some nice people will meet me in a place called England, and I will stay with them for a short time and then he and Mutti will come for me. I like trains, but I ask, "Who will look after me, who will tell me where to get off, and why can't we all go together?" Papa picks me up and puts me on his knee. He says, "This is how it must be, and you have to be a good boy and do what the ladies on the train tell you to do. You're not a baby any more, but a big boy of seven."[3]

England

In February 1939, Kurt Fuchel stood on the dock in Harwich, England. Except for the cardboard number around his neck, he was lost and alone in the crowd of children. The sights, smells, and sounds were all new to him. He could not understand what people were saying. He clutched his suitcase and shivered in the cold. In time, a friendly couple came to his side.

Kurt's British foster parents were Percy and Mariam Cohen. Percy worked in a family-owned business, making women's coats.

Henry Schmelzer wore this numbered identification tag when he went from Austria to England on a Kindertransport in December 1938. Kurt Fuchel had to wear an ID tag on his journey to England.

Mariam took care of their five-year-old son. A short time before, a shoe salesman from Vienna had come to their city of Norwich. He had gathered together everyone he could and told them what was happening in Germany and Austria. He showed pictures of the children. The Cohens wished they could take more, but they thought they could afford to care for only one child. When they got to the boat, they already knew Kurt's name and number. He recalled what happened next:

> They took me back home. I remember walking into their house. At the entrance stood the maid . . . and halfway up the stairs sat John, this little boy of five, looking at his new brother.
>   I guess I was scared, but after I came in, I was taken upstairs. My grubby clothes after three days of travel were torn off me—burned, I learned later—and I was scrubbed from head to toe, and dressed in English clothes. Then the family got together for a chicken dinner, and that I remember. That's a language I could understand. And I started to feel more at ease.[4]

Belonging

The Cohens wanted Kurt to feel like he fit in. They had an elderly German neighbor tutor him in English. The man frightened him, reminding him of the German takeover of

Children disembark from a ship in Harwich on December 12, 1938, after leaving Vienna on a children's transport. Kurt Fuchel walked on the same dock a few months later, waiting to be picked up by the Cohens.

his homeland. He consciously paid close attention to his lessons, hoping to quickly be free of his need of this tutor.

Kurt picked up the language easily. Besides his tutor, he had English lessons in school. And he had John. Only two years apart, Kurt and John played, fought, teased, and helped each other. His foster mother commented: "[Kurt] was very bright, and very popular. He just fitted in. John was only five when Kurt came. He was only a little boy, but they got along like a house on fire. Absolutely. . . . They were great, great friends. Brothers!"[5]

The Cohens treated Kurt as though he had always been part of their family . . . and always would be. Nevertheless, Kurt had a nagging concern. As time went on, he thought less and less about his parents. He wondered if he would have to leave his newfound family. Circumstances had torn him away from his first family. Could some event pull him away from the Cohens? What if he did something to displease Uncle Percy and Aunt Mariam? Would they send him away? Kurt did his best to make sure that would never happen. He was a model child.

Fear was not the only motivation Kurt had for being a good son. He knew the Cohens genuinely loved him. They had accepted him into their hearts as well as their home. And he loved them, too. Gradually, he learned to feel that he did, indeed, belong. He became an Englishman.

But what of his parents? The ones who gave up their only child to save his life? Sadly, most Kinders' parents perished during the Holocaust. His parents, however, had managed to escape.

Eva Rosenbaum (back left) goes camping with her foster family in England. Foster families welcomed many Kinder after they arrived in England. Kurt Fuchel quickly became a part of the Cohen family.

They had fled to Italy, and from there to France. But they could not get to England.

At first, Kurt and his parents were able to exchange letters. Uncle Percy made sure that Kurt wrote to his parents. After about two years, however, Kurt's parents were forced to go into hiding in France, and their letters stopped coming.

In 1945, the war ended and Kurt's parents wanted their son back. But they had nothing—no home, no job, and no plan for the future. Kurt still had two more years left of his education.

Together, the two families decided that Kurt would finish his schooling in England while his parents put their lives back together. Then he would return to his family.

Reunion

When the reunion finally took place, Kurt was sixteen. He dreaded the meeting. He had not seen his parents in eight years. He didn't really know them. He was leaving the people who had been his family since he was seven. But he was old enough to understand his parents' pain and sacrifice. He knew he was their hope, their reason for living through terrible hardships. The Cohens took him to Paris, a jumble of emotions. He later recalled:

> I didn't want to go. . . . We went to dinner in a restaurant, and I remember it was difficult because I didn't speak German or French, and they spoke very little English. I had the Cohens on one side, my parents on the other. I felt caught in the middle.[6]

The transition to "normal" family life was hard on everyone. Kurt had never seen his foster father cry, but he wept openly at their parting. Kurt's mother seemed to want to treat her teenage son as if he were still seven. His father struggled, too. But they had the rest of their lives to work the awkwardness out.

Just as he had become English, Fuchel now became French. He served in the French army, rising to the rank of officer. But his parents wanted to start completely new. They wanted to put their broken past far behind them. They applied for immigration to the United States. In 1956, the family of three sailed past the Statue of Liberty to yet another country. Fuchel, age twenty-five, became an American.

Fuchel's experience is exactly what the architects of the Kindertransport envisioned. He was taken in by a loving family, a Jewish family. He adapted well and thrived in England. His parents survived, and he reunited with them. They all made new lives for themselves after the war. He loved and maintained contact with both his families. It was the way it was supposed to work.

But not every story had a happy ending.

A Bittersweet Rescue: Bertha Engelhard Leverton

t age fifteen, Bertha Engelhard was old enough to understand the differences between Jews and Gentiles. She lived in an Orthodox Jewish family, so she grew up following the religious traditions. With her parents and younger brother and sister, she went to synagogue every Saturday and on holy days. Other people in her neighborhood went to church on Sundays. There were differences, but they were small, and everyone got along.

She was also old enough to understand that some people were prejudiced against Jews. She lived in Munich, the city in which Hitler had begun his rise to power. For five years, she had felt his antisemitic restrictions tighten. Her father's leather goods store had been forced out of business. She had been removed from the school where she was taunted and was placed in a Jewish school. As the granddaughter of Polish Jews, she understood that persecution was a fact of her existence.

But she would never understand the violence of Kristallnacht. She could not comprehend that firemen would stop fires from spreading to some buildings but allow synagogues to burn. She was shocked by the vandalism and the looting. She did understand—as did her parents—that her only hope of survival was to leave Germany.

A portrait of fifteen-year-old Bertha Engelhard, a few months before leaving Germany on a Kindertransport.

A Secret

Bertha's parents, like so many other Jews, had waited too long. They had thought this persecution, like so many in Jewish history, would pass. By the Night of Broken Glass, they had no money and no way of escape.

But one day, Bertha's ten-year-old sister brought the family a ray of hope. Bertha recalled, "She went to play with a friend and came home telling us a secret that her little friends were going to England. So my Mother said that was ridiculous, I mean England, who dreamt of England?"[1]

Bertha's father wondered if the secret could be true:

My father went around quickly to the friend's parents. They weren't very happy to tell him about it. They were told to keep it quiet. After my father found out, he went to the Jewish welfare department and said he wanted a place for his children on the Kindertransport. My father was very insistent. He said, "If you don't give me a place, I'm going to tell all my friends about it." Finally, they gave him two places for my brother and myself. My sister Inge was younger, though, and they said they couldn't possibly take more than two children from one family. We were very, very lucky.[2]

Bertha and Inge Engelhard play with pigeons in their hometown of Munich, Germany, sometime in 1937. Young Inge was the first to learn about the Kindertransport when she went to visit a friend.

Bertha's parents played up the adventure of the trip and played down the sorrow of separation. It would be only for a short time, they promised.

The Journey

So Bertha packed the one suitcase and backpack she was allowed. She went with her family to the office of the Jewish committee. Only about twenty children were going, mostly friends from her school. Other parents were crying, but Bertha's mother and father remained calm. Inge fought tears, but their parents appeared cheerful. It is a wonderful adventure, they insisted. They would soon be there, too.

So on the cold, dark night of January 4, 1939, less than two months after Kristallnacht, Bertha and her brother, Theo, boarded the train. It had come from Vienna with children from Austria. It would pick up more refugees in Frankfurt and in Berlin—all children.

At some point during the three-day trip, the sense of adventure started to fade. Homesickness set in and fear quickly took over. Bertha recalled:

> We . . . became very nervous. . . . We were very subdued. We didn't laugh and shout like children going on holiday. It was a subdued lot of children on those transports. But after we crossed the border into Holland, there was absolute joy and . . . we broke out into songs.[3]

Holland was wonderful. Colorfully dressed Dutch women greeted the children with delicious food and welcome laughter. They took the littlest ones on their laps and soothed all their worries. They rode the train with them from the border of Germany to the Hook of Holland, where a British ferry was waiting for them.

The sense of excitement returned to Bertha. She had never been to the ocean, and it was a magnificent sight. The adventure soon soured again, however, as the rolling waves made her seasick. Eventually, she was able to sleep, and she woke up in England.

Dovercourt

The Kinder who came to England fell into two groups. One group had sponsors. The sponsors knew the children's names and were prepared to take them into their homes. Kurt Fuchel was in this group. These children were taken from the dock at Harwich to the Liverpool Street Station in London and matched with their foster parents.

The second group did not have sponsors. The refugee committees had raised money to cover their transportation to the country and the required 50-pound bond, but they were still recruiting sponsors. The children in this group were taken to reception camps until they could be placed. Bertha and Theo went to Dovercourt, the largest camp.

It was a summer camp without heat or running water. Bertha and her brother arrived in winter:

> *It was bitter cold. It was one of the coldest winters in history in England and we were placed in little chalets for two or four and the icicles were inside the chalets. It was terrible, we were supplied with hot water bottles every night.*[4]

Despite the cold, their British hosts made the camp a bright spot for the children, who had been uprooted from all that was familiar. They brought groups in to entertain them and teach

Jewish children listen to their teacher as they learn English in the refugee camp at Dovercourt. Kinder who had no foster parents went to reception camps until they were placed with a family. Bertha and her brother, Theo, went to Dovercourt in January 1939.

them English. They cooked warm and wonderful food. They put on concerts and dances. It was not home, but it was caring and it was safe.

The refugee committee worked to find homes for the children. Frequently, sponsors came to Dovercourt to pick out children. Bertha thought of this selection as a cattle market. It happened every weekend. The refugees dressed in the nicest clothes they had brought in their little suitcases and sat around tables in the camp meeting hall. The visitors observed them from a distance, then called certain ones out to view them more closely. Most of the visitors seemed to want young children.

Bertha celebrated her sixteenth birthday in the camp and was becoming anxious. Her brother had been chosen by a sponsor from the city of Coventry. Then her turn came: "[Someone] asked me if I'd like to go to a family in Coventry. I jumped at the chance. I wanted to be near my little brother."[5] When the couple she came to call Uncle Billy and Aunty Vera came to pick her up, she was thrilled to go with them.

Coventry

But the thrill wore off quickly. The childless couple did not really want a daughter; they wanted a maid. They even tried to dress her in a maid's uniform. Bertha became a slave, scrubbing floors and serving tea. She remembered:

> Aunty Vera . . . resented my youth and my good health. She tormented us in many different ways, little unkindnesses, things which hurt me very much at the time. I had no new clothes while I was there. . . . To me, as a teenager, that was tragic. . . . I felt like Cinderella, which I was.[6]

The worst torture was that she was not allowed to go to school. Bertha wanted to learn, and she loved nothing more than reading. However, her new home did not have a single book.

She learned English by listening to the radio, one of the few pleasures she was permitted.

Bertha put up with the abuse for one reason: She needed to get her sister out of Germany. She had heard on the radio about the horrible things the Nazis were doing to her country. She wanted her sister safe with her. Her hosts had given refuge to one child; perhaps they would take another. She showed them a picture of Inge and begged them to sponsor her, too. Whether they wanted another servant or liked the idea of having a little girl, they said yes.

Bertha wrote to her parents and sister. The Red Cross was able to deliver mail for refugees. They had postcards on which they could write twenty-five words. In her short notes, Bertha lied about how wonderful her life in England was. These convinced her parents to send Inge on one of the Kindertransports that were now leaving Munich regularly. The ten-year-old girl arrived in the summer of 1939, about six months after Bertha. Six weeks later, the war started.

The war complicated Bertha's difficult life. In 1942, all communication from warring countries stopped, and she no longer heard from her parents. Cities in England were bombed, and Coventry was a frequent target, so Uncle Billy moved the family to Yorkshire. By then, Theo had come to live with them because his sponsor's son had become jealous of him. The refugee committee gave the hosts a little money to house him, and Theo gave them the money he earned at his job.

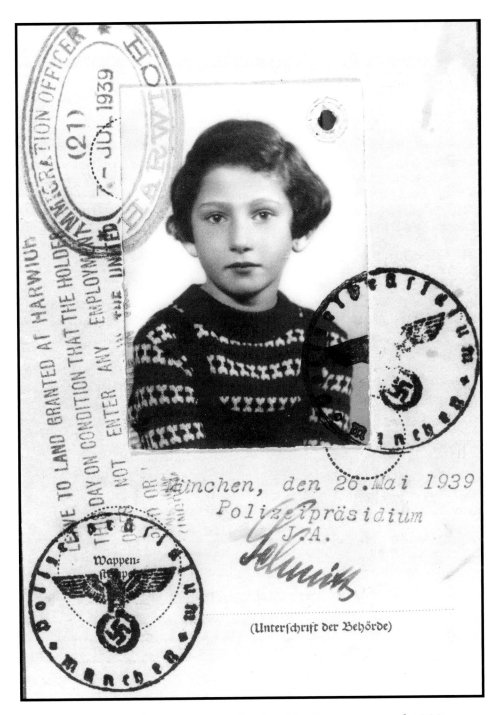

Bertha's sister, Inge, came to England in the summer of 1939. Inge traveled with this identification card in lieu of a passport after the German police revoked her citizenship.

The English city of Coventry was industrial, with car, plane, and weapons factories. The factories made the city a prime target of German bombing raids in World War II. In July and August 1940, several raids killed a number of civilians. These raids were called "blitzes," short for *blitzkrieg*, the German word meaning "lightning war."

The biggest raid occurred on the night of November 14, 1940. The Nazis nick-named the attack "Moonlight Sonata." They needed a moonlit night to carry it off.

At 7 P.M., air-raid sirens warned the citizens that planes had been spotted in the distance. People turned off their lights, drew their curtains, and closed their black-out blinds. They hid in basements and air-raid shelters. Mrs. Wyn Martin Calcott, eight years old in 1940, remembered what happened next:

Immediately following the sirens came the whistling of falling incendiary bombs. They had a whistle all of their own and from experience we recognised them.

It was necessary to extinguish the bombs as the fires which they caused helped the bombers to locate their targets. I went out, collecting my shovel to pour sand on any incendiaries likely to cause a fire. Those burning in the street were ignored.

A bomb was burning by the garage door of a house. I started to sand the bomb, suddenly the bomb exploded. The sand poured into my face and I was knocked around. All I could think was "I'm still alive."[7]

Mrs. Calcott was fortunate. In the eleven-hour blitz, five hundred tons of high explosives were unleashed in more than thirty thousand bombs. The city center and much of the outskirts were ablaze. Sixty thousand buildings, including the Coventry Cathedral of St. Michael, lay in rubble. At least 568 civilians, perhaps as many as 1,000, were dead. The devastation was so great that the Nazis invented a new word—*Coventriert* (Coventrate). It means to totally destroy.

Bertha had a job at a cotton mill, and she could have moved out of her Cinderella existence. But Uncle Billy and Aunty Vera refused to let Inge leave, and Bertha felt responsible for her. So she stayed.

Rescued Again

Bertha's world became bright again with the arrival of a telegram in January 1944. Her parents had escaped from Germany!

They had traveled through Portugal and Spain and finally reached England. They would be in Yorkshire on her twenty-first birthday.

"That was the most wonderful day of our lives!" Bertha said.[8] In the five years they were apart, Inge had forgotten most of her German. Theo spoke English far better than his native language. Their parents were older, tired, and beaten down. But all five were together at last, and that was joyous.

The children had vowed to keep their ordeal secret, but Bertha ended up sobbing the entire story to her mother the first night they were together. Her parents were outraged. They had not sent their children to freedom to have them enslaved in a home. They immediately contacted the refugee committee.

The Council House in Coventry, England, remains standing among rubble after the Nazi "blitz" of the town in November 1940. Bertha's foster family was forced to move to Yorkshire due to the constant bombing of Coventry.

The scene that followed was most unpleasant. There were accusations and denials, shouts and tears. Bertha was called a liar and a fool. But her parents held their ground. When it was over, all three children were removed from Uncle Billy and Aunty Vera's charge. The family settled in Birmingham, England, where refugees had formed a small Jewish community.

Fifty Years Later

Even as a young woman, Bertha Engelhard Leverton understood that her story was not the norm. She knew that many of the Kinder had wonderful, loving foster parents. She understood that as miserable as her experience in Coventry was, the alternative was torture and death in Nazi Germany.

Years later, in her London home, she was admiring pictures of her grandchildren. One was fifteen. She was struck by the thought that this child knew nothing about the trip her grandmother had taken at fifteen. Most of the Kinder did not talk about their past. That thought led to the first large reunion of the Kinder in London in 1989. Other reunions followed. As Bertha met other former refugees and learned more stories, she determined to preserve the memory of the tiny but inspirational slice of history. With her sister, she founded the Reunion of Kinder and edited a collection of 250 stories titled *I Came Alone*.

New Brothers and Sisters: The Attenborough Family

The Attenborough boys were privileged. Their father was the principal of University College in Leicester, England. Their mother was involved in charitable and social causes. The sons were destined for greatness. John became an executive in the Alfa Romeo automobile company, and his two older brothers were knighted by the queen. Middle son David gained fame as a natural scientist. His popular natural history television programs were seen in many countries. The eldest, Richard, became an actor, director, and producer with two Academy Awards, three Golden Globes, and numerous other prizes to his credit. But in 1938, they were mere schoolboys, more interested in soccer and cricket than anything else.

Their father, Frederick, was chairman of one of the refugee committees. He was actively involved in helping Jews escape Nazi Germany. The refugees generally had relatives in Canada or the United States, but they could not go directly there from Germany. Committee members housed them in England for a few days while their documents were processed and transportation arranged.

Two German Sisters

That is how Irene and Helga Bejach came to the Attenboroughs. Their mother had died, and their father, a medical officer in

A group of Jewish men line up after being arrested in Germany during Kristallnacht on November 10, 1938. They are awaiting deportation to Dachau. Irene and Helga Bejach's father was detained at Dachau after Kristallnacht.

Berlin, was a Jew. His home had been destroyed by gun-wielding brutes on Kristallnacht, and he had been arrested and taken to a concentration camp. His daughters were *Mischlings*—half Jewish. In Hitler's Germany, any Jewish blood was enough to mark a person for persecution and eventual death. After being released from the camp, the girls' father contacted relatives in America; they agreed to let the sisters live with them. In August 1939, he sent Irene, age twelve, and Helga, age ten, on a Kindertransport.

"I will never forget when Helga and Irene first arrived at our home," Richard Attenborough said many years later. "Two pale waifs with their pathetic little suitcases."[1]

Richard, who was just turning sixteen; David, thirteen; and John, eleven, were used to sharing their home with temporary guests. Other people had enjoyed their parents' hospitality as they made their way to more permanent housing. But three weeks after the girls came to Leicester, Germany invaded Poland. Flights for refugees to the United States were halted. It looked like Irene and Helga would be staying longer than a few days.

Frederick and Mary called their three sons into their father's study: "We think we ought to adopt them," they explained, even though the adoption would be only temporary. "But we need your agreement," they continued. "There'll be fewer holidays, fewer outings. We'll be a family of seven, instead of a family of five."[2]

Mary pressed, to be certain the boys understood:

> *Darlings, this will be very difficult for you and maybe you will be jealous and that will be very understandable. Your father and I are devoted to you and give you all our love, but I will now have to find even more love for these two girls because they have nothing, nobody at all. I must be their mother in terms of love and devotion and it is possible you will find it hurtful.[3]*

In the end, she let the boys decide: "It is entirely up to you, darlings, if they stay."[4]

The boys did not even consider saying no. Their parents had always modeled kindness to them—kindness to one another and to any who were less fortunate. Richard later remembered, "We all said we thought it was a marvelous idea: for three boys suddenly to have two sisters in the family was very good luck."[5]

Becoming Family

As fun and as noble as the idea seemed, getting to know two homesick, non-English-speaking strangers was not easy. The girls kept to themselves, and they cried quite a lot at first. And even though they were ten and twelve, they reverted to the childhood habit of wetting the bed. It would take much time, patience, and love before they would feel secure in the unfamiliar surroundings.

As the weeks turned to months, Irene and Helga grew more comfortable in the Attenborough home. They went to school. They learned the language and took part in school activities. "We did everything together," Richard wrote later. "There were little jealousies, little quarrels, as with any kids, but we came to love each other very much."[6]

As the months turned to years, the girls' individual personalities and interests emerged. Irene, like David, relished studying. Helga liked

Richard Attenborough was sixteen years old when Helga and Irene came to stay with his family. Richard (center) became a famous actor and director; he is seen here during the filming of a movie called *Son of a Gun* in November 1955.

to dance. Richard would often amuse his sisters with lines from some play he was rehearsing. John sewed sequins on Helga's ballet dresses. They had become family.

But no matter how wonderful the Attenboroughs were, Irene and Helga longed for their father. The war ended, and still they heard nothing from him. Finally, a letter came from the Red Cross. It traced their father's history from the time they bade him farewell in Berlin. He had been forced to serve as a doctor in a Nazi slave labor camp. From there, he was deported to the Theresienstadt camp in Czechoslovakia. He was listed as part of a transport that was then shipped to Auschwitz. That is where the history ended.

Remaining Family

The Red Cross letter was devastating. The two girls wept as they realized that their family in Germany was completely gone. But they still had their English family. They would always have the Attenboroughs.

In 1946, they resumed the journey that was interrupted seven years earlier; they went to their relatives in the United States. They married and had families. Despite the miles between them, their English family remained a strong part of their lives. In fact, when Samuel Goudsmit, a world-renowned physics professor, proposed to Irene, she would not say yes until he had flown to England and asked Uncle Frederick's permission.

Over the years, the five Attenborough children visited back and forth between the two countries. Richard's film career took

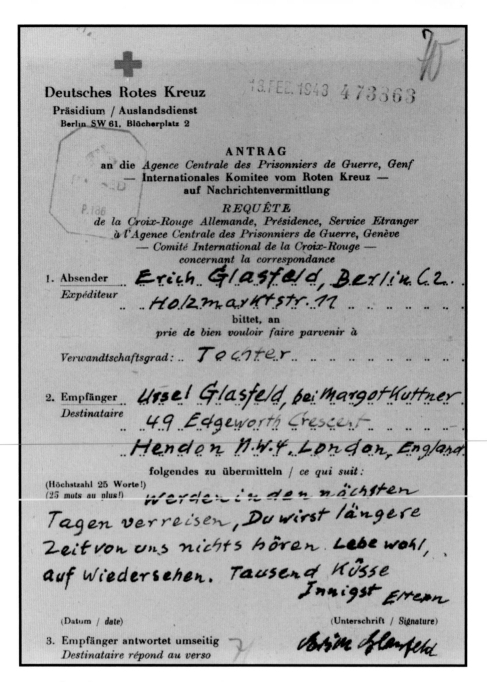

Deutsches Rotes Kreuz

Präsidium / Auslandsdienst
Berlin SW 61, Blücherplatz 2

13. FEB. 1943 473363

ANTRAG
an die *Agence Centrale des Prisonniers de Guerre, Genf*
— Internationales Komitee vom Roten Kreuz —
auf Nachrichtenvermittlung

REQUÊTE
de la Croix-Rouge Allemande, Présidence, Service Étranger
à l'Agence Centrale des Prisonniers de Guerre, Genève
— Comité International de la Croix-Rouge —
concernant la correspondance

1. Absender *Erich Glasfeld, Berlin C.2.*
   Expéditeur *Holzmarktstr. 11*

bittet, an
prie de bien vouloir faire parvenir à

Verwandtschaftsgrad: *Tochter*

2. Empfänger *Ursel Glasfeld, bei Margot Huttner*
   Destinataire *49 Edgeworth Crescent*
   Hendon N.W.4. London, England

folgendes zu übermitteln / *ce qui suit:*
(Höchstzahl 25 Worte!)
(25 mots au plus!) *Werden in den nächsten*
Tagen verreisen, Du wirst längere
Zeit von uns nichts hören. Lebe wohl,
auf Wiedersehen. Tausend Küsse
Innigst Eltern

(Datum / *date*)   (Unterschrift / *Signature*)

3. Empfänger antwortet umseitig
   Destinataire répond au verso

Erich Glasfeld wrote this Red Cross letter to his daughter, Ursel, shortly before he and his wife were deported to Theresienstadt, where he died. Ursel had gone to London on one of the last Kindertransports on August 22, 1939. Helga and Irene received a Red Cross letter while living with the Attenboroughs in England notifying them of their father's death.

him to the United States often, and he nearly always saw his sisters when he came. The girls traveled to England for special occasions. They kept up with one another through phone conversations, cards, and letters. The girls attended premieres of Richard's movies, and the boys were proud of Helga's work with the Florida Holocaust Museum. They remained brothers and sisters until Irene died in 1992 and Helga in 2005.

Jewish refugee children wave at the Statue of Liberty upon their arrival in New York City. Helga and Irene went to live with their relatives in the United States after the war ended.

Enemy Alien: Walter Kohn

Walter Kohn's story begins like those of thousands of others. He was born into a patriotic Jewish family in Vienna, Austria. His early childhood was happy, filled with grandparents and cousins, art and music, and summers on the Baltic Sea. Then came the Anschluss, the melding of Austria into Nazi Germany. And life changed. His father lost his business, he was expelled from school, and his former friends mistreated him. His parents found a spot for Walter and his sister on a Kindertransport.

The story of Walter's family ends like most of the others. His parents and the rest of his relatives who stayed in Austria were murdered in the Nazi gas chambers.

Like many of the Kinder, Walter and his sister were sponsored. Walter wrote of his British sponsors:

> After having been separated from my parents who were unable to leave Austria, I was taken into the homes of . . . Charles and Eva Hauff in Sussex, England, who also welcomed my older sister, Minna. Charles, like my father, was in art publishing and they had a business relationship.[1]

Walter was one of the older Kinder, sixteen when he arrived on one of the last transports. He had decided that he did not want to go to school in England. His parents were well educated, but they had lost their jobs. Artists, scientists, and teachers in Austria were out of work. He figured if he learned something more practical, he would have a better chance of surviving in a cruel world. He wanted to become a farmer.

That opportunity was available to him. The county of Kent, in the southeast corner of England, had a training farm. It offered young men thirteen and older an introduction to farmwork. In an

This is a group portrait of members of the Ezra youth movement working at a training farm outside London. Most of the boys in the group came to England on a Kindertransport. Walter Kohn went to a training farm in Kent when he arrived in England.

eight-week training period, the boys planted, tended, or harvested crops. They plowed fields, milked cows, and drove tractors. They broke, groomed, and worked horses. When their training ended, they were qualified for paying jobs on other farms.

Walter did not last the full eight weeks because he contracted meningitis. The illness turned out to be a good thing for Walter. The Hauffs brought him back to their home and enrolled him in the East Grinstead County School in Sussex. There, he fell in love with mathematics, physics, and chemistry. Walter was still in school when his story took a turn much different from that of most of the other Kinder.

Arrested

England had declared war on Germany two days after Germany invaded Poland, just days after Walter escaped. As soon as war was declared, England's leaders looked nervously on the Germans living among them. They feared that some of the foreigners might help the Nazis. They could even be spies. The leaders classified everyone from a foreign country as an "alien." Any people from a country with which Britain was at war were called "enemy aliens." In September 1939, about eighty thousand people in England were from Germany or Austria.

All male enemy aliens ages sixteen to sixty had to register. They were placed in one of three categories. About six hundred fell into Category A, high security risk. They were immediately interned—held in special camps. Sixty-five hundred were considered low risk and consigned to Category B. They were not interned, but they were watched and their movements were restricted. All the rest, in Category C, were deemed to be no risk at all. They were "friendly enemy aliens." Fifty-five thousand of these were refugees; most were Jewish. Walter was a Category C enemy alien.

For the first year and a half of the war, alien status meant little. Almost no fighting was going on during this period that was known as the "phony war." But in the spring of 1940, Germany launched a sudden blitzkrieg against the West. With lightning speed, the German army crashed across Western Europe. One by one, Denmark, Norway, Belgium, Luxembourg, the Netherlands, and France fell. England was the only nation left to fight the German war machine. It looked like that machine, which had swallowed so many, was poised to invade England.

The people and leaders of Britain were jittery. The new prime minister, Winston Churchill, met with his War Cabinet to determine how to defend the island country. The subject of enemy aliens arose. What should they do about the possible spies in their midst? They had already arrested and interned all the Category As. What of the others? Churchill decided to play it safe. He issued the order, "Collar the lot!"[2] Arrest all of them, every male with a German or Austrian passport between the ages of sixteen and sixty.

So in May 1940, just after his seventeenth birthday, Walter was taken into custody. He was one of a thousand Kinder interned as enemy aliens.

FORM R.

NYASALAND PROTECTORATE.

DRIVING PERMIT.

(Motor Traffic Ordinance, No. 1 of 1934.)

This is to certify that..............................

.......KALMAN HABER..............

of................ZOMBA..................

whose photograph, signature or thumb ... have ... been placed hereon, having been tes... and fo... competent, is permitted to drive............

..............*Private Cars*...........

.... The following ... restrictions........ ....

D...at Zomba on ... Nov. ... 1943

... C. Meathen ...

(Signature of Licensing Officer.)

26 NOV 1943

REGISTRAR OF MOTOR VEHICLES 1943 · NYASALAND

(Signature or thumbmark of holder.)

In May 1940, Walter Kohn was interned as an enemy alien. Britain had all males between the ages of sixteen and sixty with German or Austrian passports interned. This driver's license was issued to Kalman Haber, an Austrian Jew, who was interned in Nyasaland (present-day Malawi, Africa) as an enemy alien.

interned

The purpose of the internment camps was not punishment. None of the enemy aliens was guilty of any crime. The purpose was to keep the aliens away from possible contact with German agents.

The internment process was sudden and disorganized. Internees were placed in hastily setup quarters on horse-racing tracks, in abandoned warehouses, and in other empty places. Two months after the order was given, Rabbi Solomon Schonfeld visited some of the camps. At Prees Heath, he observed, "Conditions were rather primitive. There was no house or hut. Internees of all kinds and ages were living in tents. The camp hospital was also under canvas. . . . The daily sick-parade was considerable. . . . The camp contained about 1,000 men."[3]

At Huyton, near Liverpool, he reported, "As yet there was practicably no furniture, although the houses and grounds provided good shelter."[4]

The rabbi saw similar problems at other camps, mostly because they were put together so quickly. But he also noted that the camp personnel were "very concerned about the welfare of the men" and "every effort was being made to alleviate suffering."[5]

People in Britain's War Office decided that enemy aliens who might truly be a threat to the country needed to be out of England. They set up internment camps in Australia, Canada, and on the Isle of Man. After being held in a series of camps in England, Kohn was transferred to one of the camps on the Isle of Man, a small piece of land in the Irish Sea between England and Northern Ireland.

Kohn found conditions there much better than in the makeshift camps. Housing and food were decent. Despite the barbed wire, internees could hike and swim. Some of the older German refugees were professors, scientists, and artists. The aliens organized "universities" and cultural activities. Even those who were not particularly studious attended "classes" because there was little else to do on the isolated island. Kohn's teachers sent him his schoolbooks, and he used the two months he was interned to study. He listened to lectures on physics and mathematics.

GERMAN U-BOATS

The name U-boat is short for the German *Unterseeboot*—undersea boat. It was a submarine used by the German military in World Wars I and II.

The Treaty of Versailles that ended World War I limited the German navy to twenty-four ships. Submarines were completely forbidden. But Germany set up "research facilities" in the Netherlands and Sweden and built underwater vessels. By the time the Second World War started, Germany had about sixty U-boats. Some were used in what Churchill called the Battle for the Atlantic.

Control of the Atlantic Ocean was crucial in the war. England could not fight without a steady supply of food, tanks, vehicles, and other equipment from North America. The German U-boat was not used as much in battle as it was employed against merchant ships carrying supplies to Great Britain.

The U-boats were powered by battery when under water and by diesel when above the surface. Under water they were slow, and their batteries limited how far they could travel. So they usually dove beneath the surface only to fire their torpedoes. The weapons were not always accurate, and they did not always explode. When they did, however, they were deadly. Churchill once wrote: "The only thing that ever really frightened me during the war was the U-Boat peril."[6]

During the course of the war, Germany made many improvements to its submarine technology. The U-boats sank close to three thousand Allied ships; almost 95 percent were merchant vessels.

U-boats posed a dangerous threat to Allied ships during World War II. This cartoon by D. R. Fitzpatrick from November 1, 1941, depicts the sinking of an American destroyer, USS *Reuben James*, by a German U-boat.

Canada

As more enemy aliens were interned, Kohn was among those moved from camp to camp:

> In July 1940, I was shipped on, as part of a British convoy moving through U-boat-infested waters, to Quebec City in Canada; and from there, by train, to a camp in Trois Rivieres, which housed both German civilian internees and refugees like myself. . . . Later I was moved around among various other camps in Quebec and New Brunswick.[7]

The Canadian camps had a little more to offer than the ones in England. Internees were given the opportunity to work. Kohn became a lumberjack, felling trees for twenty cents a day. He used the money to buy mathematics and physics handbooks.

As in England, the camps offered excellent schooling. PhDs from some of the most prestigious universities in Vienna and Britain were interned with Kohn. He was able to finish his high school education in the camps and get a good start on college.

Not long after Kohn arrived in Canada, two tragic incidents halted the detention of enemy aliens. The *Arandora Star*, bound for Canada with almost fifteen hundred internees, was sunk by German torpedoes. A week later, the *Dunera* set sail for Australia. Cruel conditions on the ship, the inhumane treatment of the foreigners onboard, and the two-month voyage sparked outrage in England. The British Parliament ordered the release of all internees.

When Kohn was freed in January 1942, he was nineteen and completely alone. His parents had both been killed at Auschwitz. He had no money, no job, and no home. A Jewish professor in Toronto, Dr. Bruno Mendel, and his wife, Hertha, invited him to become part of their family. Mendel was from the Netherlands. He had managed to get out of the country before the Nazis came. Mendel knew firsthand what it was like to be an outcast because of Nazism. Kohn was one of five refugees who lived with the Mendels.

Walter Kohn (left) receives the Nobel Prize in Chemistry from Swedish King Carl Gustaf XVI in Stockholm, Sweden.

Physicist

Dr. Mendel helped Kohn enroll in the University of Toronto. Kohn wanted to study, but the war was still on, and he also wanted to fight the armies that had forced him out of Austria. When he was accepted into the Canadian army, he suspended his studies to serve the country that had taken him in.

After his tour of duty, he returned to the university. Kohn became a world-renowned scientist and eventually settled in the United States. In 1998, he was awarded the Nobel Prize in Chemistry. When he wrote his autobiography, as Nobel Prize recipients do, he attributed his success to his experiences that began with the Kindertransport:

> I note with deep gratitude that twice, during the Second World War . . . I was taken into the homes of two wonderful families who had never seen me before. . . . I cannot imagine how I might have become a scientist without their help.[8]

Kohn dedicated his research to people like his parents, who did not live through the Holocaust:

> A person, like myself, who . . . loses a lot of really close relatives . . . they automatically have a sense of carrying the lost relatives on his shoulders. I feel like I'm doing this work not only on my own behalf but on the behalf of people who didn't make it.[9]

Most of the Kinder were wrenched away from their families at the train platforms; Abrascha Gorbulski never had much of a family. When he was three, his father died. His brother was nearly ten years older than he, so they were not particularly close. His mother, without a husband to help her, placed her children in a Jewish orphanage when Abrascha was seven. She loved them and communicated with them. She just could not work and care for two children at the same time. Abrascha had relatives in America, but he did not know them. He was really all alone.

When Abrascha graduated from high school, he had to leave the orphanage. What could he do? There were not many prospects for a young Jewish boy in Hamburg, Germany, in 1938. Someone at the orphanage told him about a farm not far from Berlin. It was part of the *aliyah* movement.

Aliyah is a Hebrew word that means "go up." Many Jews in the 1930s dreamed of "going up" to Palestine. Palestine, the site of the ancient kingdom of Israel, was a territory of Great Britain at that time. Britain allowed a trickle of Jews to immigrate there. A number of Jewish organizations in different European countries were preparing young Jews to move to Palestine. Boys and girls his age would work on farms for two years and then apply for a visa to Palestine.

Abrascha was Jewish, but he was not particularly religious. Still, Palestine looked a lot better to him than Nazi Germany at that moment. Besides, his brother had already gone to Palestine. Maybe they could be a family there. He applied for the training program and was accepted.

Close Calls

Abrascha was reasonably comfortable on the farm. It was not terribly different from living at the orphanage. He had been there about six months when Gestapo agents came. They lined up all

Three young Jews take care of a cow at a training farm in Gross Breesen, Germany. Abrascha Gorbulski went to a training farm, where young men learned the skills they would need to live in Palestine.

the youths with Polish backgrounds and piled them into cars. There was not enough room for all of them, and Abrascha was left behind. He learned later that the others were taken to a train in Berlin that dumped them at the Polish border. He had narrowly missed the first deportation of Polish Jews from Germany.

His mother was not as fortunate:

> They came to my mother's apartment at five o'clock in the morning. The Gestapo liked to do things early in the morning when it was very quiet on the street so nobody would notice. They told her to get dressed, come outside, and bingo, she was taken away.[1]

Abrascha's mother survived in Poland at least until the start of the war; she wrote often to her son. But in September 1939, the letters stopped:

> After the Germans marched in [to Poland], I never heard another thing. Total silence. . . . At the end of the war, I tried to find out what happened, but whatever family was left in Poland all disappeared. I was the last one in the family to get out.[2]

Abrascha had another close call on Kristallnacht. The houses on the farm did not escape the terrible violence of that night.

When Abrascha and his companions heard gunshots break the windows of their building, they bolted outside. All night long they hid among the crops in the fields. At the first light of dawn, they crept back, only to find the houses in ruins. One of the rioters was still there. He ordered the youths to leave at once and threatened to kill them if they came back.

Once again, Abrascha was alone with no place to go. He went back to Hamburg, to the offices of the Jewish organization. The Jewish community was the closest thing he had to a family. A woman on the committee told him about a train that was taking children to England. Abrascha was sixteen, barely under the age limit.

England

On December 14, 1938, Abrascha boarded one of the very first Kindertransports. No one went to the station with him. No one sat with him on the train. When he reached England, he was not greeted by a sponsoring family.

Because he had no sponsor, Abrascha went with other boys his age to a hostel: "We arrived in Harwich and were taken to a holiday [summer] camp at Lowestoft that had no heat. It was raining, freezing cold, and we were in these little huts."[3]

Abrascha was so miserable that when a call came for volunteers to move to another hostel, he jumped at the chance.

The second hostel, in Leeds, was not ready for the fifty German children who were to be housed there, so the refugee committee put them up briefly in a hotel. The refugees were treated to swimming

HOSTELS

Placing ten thousand children in homes in nine months was no easy task; in fact, it was impossible. In order to house the many Kinder who did not have foster parents waiting for them, the British rescue committees set up youth hostels—group homes—for many of the refugees. They used whatever buildings they could find: large houses in London and other cities, Gwrych Castle in northern Wales, the massive Whittingehame Estate of Lord Balfour in Scotland.

In the hostels in the cities, some of the Kinder learned trades, such as carpentry. In the countryside, they learned farming. Many were old enough to work, and some found jobs, usually performing manual labor, farming, or in domestic service.

The Jewish organization Youth Aliyah set up hostels and training farms for the refugees. Leaders of Youth Aliyah taught young men and women to farm in the hopes that they could eventually emigrate to Palestine.

The refugee committees did what they could for the displaced youth, but the children who were from Orthodox families struggled. They missed the Jewish customs and did not want to eat food that was not prepared as prescribed by Jewish traditions. Solomon Schonfeld, a British rabbi who rescued thousands of Jews, established some Jewish hostels and schools for these Kinder.

The hostels may not have been the ideal placement the refugee committees had hoped for, but they provided housing, training, care, and safety. One resident of Gwrych Castle summed up their value: "For the first time, we were treated like human beings, equal to everyone else. This place gave us a new life and we really felt what it meant to be free. We will be eternally grateful to the Welsh people for that."[4]

parties, movies, and performances. But it still felt more like an orphanage than like a family.

Eventually, Abrascha was moved again, this time to a home in London. Because he was sixteen, he was able to find a job. A year and a half later, two policemen came to his work site. Abrascha was caught in the arrest of enemy aliens.

Like Walter Kohn, Abrascha was shuffled between temporary detention facilities. He spent a few days at the Kempton Park racecourse and a few days in the tents at Huyton. That is where his story diverged from those of most of the other Kinder. A call went out for single men to volunteer to go to Canada.

At first, Gorbulski was reluctant. Just a few days earlier, he and all England had heard the news of the *Arandora Star*. The ship, carrying refugees to Canada, had been sunk by the Germans, and more than seven hundred people had lost their lives. But his concern for his safety was eclipsed by a stronger force. Canada was close to the United States, and he had relatives in America. Perhaps he could finally find the family he always longed for.

Jewish children attend a Hanukkah party at a hostel in Margate, England. Many Kinder, like Abrascha Gorbulski, stayed in hostels if they had no sponsor.

The *Dunera*

Thus on July 10, 1940, Gorbulski boarded the *Dunera* in Liverpool, England. In all, more than seven thousand enemy aliens were sent overseas, including about four hundred Kinder. Most were treated decently. The experience of those on the *Dunera* was the exception.

The troopship was designed to carry a maximum of fifteen hundred, including the crew. But the leaders of England feared an imminent invasion, and they were anxious to remove anyone who might aid the enemy. More than twenty-five hundred men were

The SS *Arandora Star*, pictured here, was sunk by a German U-boat killing many refugees onboard. This event made Gorbulski feel reluctant to take the *Dunera*.

herded onto the ship. A few were German and Italian prisoners of war who might indeed be dangerous. The majority, however, were Jewish refugees from Nazi oppression. They included the eight hundred survivors of the *Arandora Star*. The 2,500 were guarded by 309 British soldiers.

From the moment they boarded the ship, the "aliens" were treated harshly. An official report called the *Dunera Memorandum* described their welcoming:

Everything carried in hand or loose in the pockets was taken off the internees. All less valuable effects like gloves, toilet utensils, eatables, pipes etc., were thrown disorderly on the ground. Valuables were stuffed into sacks or disappeared openly into the pockets of the soldiers. Soon rows of empty wallets were lying on the floor, the contents of emptied attaché cases were roughly thrown about. . . . Valuable documents, identity and emigration papers, testimonials of all kinds, were taken away, thrown on the ground or even . . . torn up before the eyes of their very owners. No receipts were given, except by one single searching party. Appeals to the officers standing by were fruitless. Attempts of protest were roughly suppressed. . . . Of all the articles taken away on the landing stage, only a very few were ever seen again.[5]

Gorbulski was directed downstairs to the third deck. It was so crowded he barely had room to move. There were not enough hammocks for everyone, so Gorbulski slept on the floor. All the portholes were covered over, toilet facilities were totally inadequate, and there was no place to wash. Because of the severe overcrowding, the men were confined to the dark, dirty, stifling hot deck for much of the voyage. "There was so little air," internee Walter Kaufmann complained, "that to get the job of peeling potatoes on deck was seen as a life-saver."[6]

When the refugees were permitted topside, the guards treated them with horrible barbarity. They taunted them, beat them, and threw their possessions overboard. They made them go barefoot the little time they were allowed on the top deck, and the soldiers broke bottles on the deck so it was littered with glass.

On the second day of the trip, Gorbulski heard a loud thud. The ship shook and the lights went out. He and the other hundreds on the third deck raced to the stairway. Only a few could elbow their way to the top. Fortunately, the lights came back on and the ship continued. Gorbulski learned later that the vessel had been hit by a torpedo, but the torpedo failed to explode.

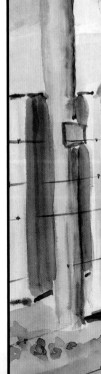

The journey that should have taken a few days stretched into weeks. At some point, the passengers concluded that they were not headed to Canada. Fifty-seven days after leaving port, the *Dunera* dropped anchor. They were in Australia!

Finding a Home

The first person aboard the ship when it docked in Sydney, Australia, was Australian medical officer Alan Frost. Disgusted by the inhumane conditions, he began procedures that ended with the court martial of the ship's commanding officer. When the reports of the mistreatment of people on the *Dunera* and the sinking of the *Arandora Star* reached London, the internment of enemy aliens was stopped.

But by that time, Gorbulski and the others were already in a camp outside Sydney. A year after the *Dunera*'s arrival in Sydney, the British government made Gorbulski an offer. He could stay where he was, behind the barbed wire of the relatively comfortable camp, or return to England and join the

The Hay Internment Camp in New South Wales, Australia, is shown in this painting by one of the internees at the camp. The so-called "enemy aliens" aboard the *Dunera* were brought to this camp. Gorbulski remained there until he joined the Alien Pioneer Corps.

Alien Pioneer Corps. The corps was an arm of the royal military. The choice was a no-brainer for Gorbulski. For one thing, Australia was too hot for a boy from northern Germany. But the main reason, he said: "I hated the Germans . . . and I wanted to be part of the war."[7]

For its first two years, the Pioneer Corps was a non-combat force composed of friendly enemy aliens. English officers could not risk the moral dilemma a German or Austrian refugee might face if he was confronted with the decision of having to shoot a fellow German or Austrian. So members of the Alien Pioneer Corps did not carry weapons. They worked in support positions, in construction or other manual labor tasks.

In 1943, the former refugees were allowed to join the fighting units. Gorbulski quickly signed on. German-speaking soldiers were especially valuable in spy work behind enemy lines and in interrogating captured German soldiers. Gorbulski fought in France, Belgium, and Germany. The foreigners who joined the military during the war anglicized their names—made them British sounding. That way, if they were captured, the Germans would hold them as POWs rather than execute them as traitors. Abrascha Gorbulski became Alexander Gordon.

Gordon remained in the service until the end of 1947. His only relatives still alive were his brother in Israel and the ones he did not know in the United States. He decided to go to America. There, he finally settled permanently. He married and had children and grandchildren. He finally found the family he always longed for . . . by creating it himself.

100

9 Two Cousins, Two Stories: Madeleine Albright and Dagmar Simova

Dagmar was nine when her cousin was born. She already had a five-year-old sister, but she was thrilled with another baby girl. Her cousin was born Marie Jana Körbelova, but everyone called her Madlenka.[1] The two were not able to be together as often as Dagmar would like. They lived more than four hundred miles apart. That was quite a distance in 1937.

Dagmar lived in Czechoslovakia, and Madlenka had moved to Yugoslavia. The year Madlenka was born, her father had started a new job. Josef Körbel, a member of the Czech Foreign Ministry, was appointed press attaché at the Czech Embassy in Belgrade, Yugoslavia. The cousins got together when Madlenka's family returned to Prague for visits.

The Körbels were in Belgrade when Hitler began to take parts of Czechoslovakia. Yugoslavia was safe from the Nazis at the moment, but Körbel's job was not. A number of people in the government of Czechoslovakia were pro-German, and Körbel was a staunch Czech patriot. And he had a larger problem: He was Jewish. In late December, less than three months after Germany annexed part of Czechoslovakia, Körbel was dismissed from his post and sent back to Prague. That is where he, his wife, and Madlenka were when Hitler's army marched into that city on March 15, 1939.

German troops pose and salute for a photo after marching into the Sudetenland region of Czechoslovakia. This territory became a dangerous place for Jews, and many began looking for a way out.

Escape

Josef's brother had seen the crisis coming. He had managed to get his family out of the country and into England before the final blow. He had sold the business that belonged to his and Josef's father and taken the money with him. But Josef had waited too long. His wife, Mandula, wrote:

> *To leave Czechoslovakia was technically impossible. There was complete chaos in Prague. Communications were stopped . . . banks were closed, friends were arrested. We learned from competent sources that Joe's name is also on some list of people who should be arrested.[2]*

As the conquering army spread out over Prague, the Körbels hid with friends, each night with someone different. Then, as Mandula later wrote, "with the help of some good friends and lots of luck and a little bribery," they got exit visas and fled to Yugoslavia, then Greece, and finally England. Josef's brother, Jan, was there to welcome them.[3]

Back in Prague, Dagmar's family was also desperate to escape. Her parents went to all the embassies, pleading for visas to England, Canada, or the United States. Their forms were buried in mountains of similar applications. Finally, in July, they got lucky. All four could not leave, but there was a spot on one of Nicholas Winton's children's trains to England. The parents decided to keep seven-year-old Milena with them and send their older daughter. Dagmar was on one of the last Kindertransports out of Prague. In England, she came to live with her cousin Madlenka.

Different Lives

The two cousins were both refugees, but their flights were totally different. Madlenka was two, hardly aware of the panic and

Dagmar Simova had to make the journey to England by herself.
In this photo, a young girl sits alone with her doll after arriving in
Harwich on the first Kindertransport on December 2, 1938.

danger around her. She had both her parents and was secure in their care. Dagmar was eleven. She left her parents, grandparents, and little sister in a train station. She made a very frightening journey alone.

The girls' experiences in England were also different. Unlike many refugees, the Körbel brothers could afford their own housing. They had the money Jan had brought with him from Czechoslovakia. They used some of that money to send Dagmar to a girls' boarding school. So while Madlenka explored the streets of London, carefree in the charge of her parents, Dagmar was with the family only when school was out. She was like a big sister who visited on holidays.

In England, Madlenka had no reason to think of Prague or anyone there. Dagmar, however, never stopped dreaming about her former life. "For six years," she said, "I had assumed that I would be going back to my family. But it turned out that there was no family to go back to."[4]

When the war was over, Dagmar and the Körbels returned to Prague, and Dagmar learned that everyone in her family—her parents, grandparents, little sister, great aunts and uncles—had perished in the Nazi camps. She was orphaned, alone. Her uncle, Madlenka's father, became her official guardian.

Körbel resumed his life almost where it had left off. He was made Czechoslovakia's ambassador to Yugoslavia. That meant moving again to Belgrade. He did not take Dagmar with him again; he found another relative to take her in. Once more,

Liebe Fränzi,

sei nicht böse, daß wir machen
so unvernünftige Sachen
wie, zum Abschied zu erscheinen!
Doch, Fränzi, wir wollen nicht
weinen!

...us für uns nur innig ist.
Wenn Du uns nicht ganz
vergißt!
Dann wir mal 'was hören von Dir
...nnen nun von uns dies
Briefpapier.

Doch machen wir drauf aufmerksam
wir Dich:
Recht oft zu schreiben ist nun Deine Pflicht!

Dagmar had to leave all her family behind when she left Prague.
Oftentimes, Kinder had no family to return to after the war, and
the only memories remaining were items brought with them.
Frances Rose received this poem before she left on the first
Kindertransport.

Madlenka went off happily with her parents, and her cousin was left almost to herself.

The Körbels' stay in Belgrade did not last long. A Communist takeover of the Yugoslav government in 1948 again put Körbel in danger. He sought political asylum in the United States for his family, which now numbered five. He did not take Dagmar.

Körbel, as an "enemy of the Communist revolution," almost certainly escaped arrest, trial, and possible death. Dagmar, on the other hand, suffered for her uncle's political loyalty. She was hauled in before a government commission and questioned about Körbel. She was expelled from the university she attended and denied employment. Unlike her cousin, she was not able to escape.

Adults

Meanwhile, Madlenka settled comfortably in the United States with an Americanized version of her name: Madeleine. Her father taught international relations at the University of Denver, and he sent Madeleine to some of the best schools in the country. She married publisher Joseph Albright and became active in politics. In 1997, President Bill Clinton appointed her the first woman U.S. secretary of state.

In the same year, a reporter unearthed the fact that Madeleine Albright's parents were Jewish. Albright was completely surprised by the revelation. "The only thing I have to go by is what my mother and father told me," she said to reporters.[5] They had told her nothing about her family's past and the reason that she had lived six years in England. They simply said her grandparents had died during the war.

Dagmar, nine years older than Madeleine, knew the truth, but for five decades the two cousins had almost never communicated. When the facts of their childhood finally came to light, Madeleine said, "My parents were fabulous people who did everything they could for their children and . . . were protective."[6]

Madeleine Albright (right) meets her cousin, Dagmar Simova, in a hotel lobby in Prague on July 14, 1997. The two cousins had not seen each other in more than fifty years.

Unlike her cousin, Dagmar lived her adult life under the oppression of Communism in Yugoslavia. Despite the hardships, she was able to say, "I don't regret anything. I have had a good life, a good marriage, a good family. My children are happy."[7]

Both cousins owe their happiness to their parents, who had the courage to take or send their daughters to safety in a tumultuous and dangerous time.

AFTERWORD

The Kinder experienced safety because of the kindness, daring, and sacrifice of others. They were spared the torturous deaths that befell 90 percent of their families, because, in most cases, complete strangers shared their resources and their homes with them.[1]

The Kinder have permanent scars—from the horrors in their homelands, the adjustment to a totally foreign culture, and the loss of family. Inge Saden, Bertha Engelhard Leverton's sister, remarked: "I think I lead a pretty normal life now, but I have no roots, and that bothers me."[2]

Her sister, speaking on behalf of all the Kinder, observed: "It was terrible and the trauma never left any of them, even to this day. They are still crying for their parents. There is no other way, you never get over a thing like that."[3]

Kurt Fuchel had his parents, but he still bore lifelong scars: "I frequently feel like an outsider, and stand apart. While I was in England, I knew that my parents might someday come and reclaim me, and, as a consequence, I have difficulty with making a 100% commitment."[4]

But the Kinder willingly carry the burden of their losses and their pain. They know only too well what the alternative was. They understand that the pain forged in them a toughness of character, an appreciation for the goodness of others, and a tenderness toward people who are hurting. Charlotte Levy, who sent her nine-year-old son from Austria to England in 1938, saw the experience develop character in both parents and children: "All those I know who have escaped the Holocaust and started a new life have done well. The deeply shaking and uprooting experience had ploughed us and brought more strength to the surface than we had attributed to ourselves."[5]

The Kindertransport saved thousands of children from certain death. This commemorative statue unveiled in Berlin, Germany, on November 30, 2008, is dedicated to preserving the memory of the Kindertransport.

One and a half million children perished in the Holocaust; the Kindertransport saved about ten thousand from that fate. It is but a fraction of the number killed. But the children and grandchildren of those ten thousand probably number more than eighty thousand today. They are all over the world, contributing positively to their communities. They include writers, professors, statesmen, and two Nobel Prize winners. They are living and

Thomas Bermann holds the identification card he used on his journey to safety in England during a ceremony marking the seventieth anniversary of the Kindertransport at Liverpool Street Station in London.

thriving today because a few people in one small country reached out to help children. Those few enlisted the help of a few more people in a few other countries. None of them could do much against the raging storm of Nazism, but each one did what he or she could. The story of the Kindertransports is a bright light in an otherwise dark part of European history, because the main characters adopted the attitude of Nicholas Winton: "I knew I could not save the world and I knew I could not stop war from coming, but I knew I could save one human soul."[6]

1938

March 12—In an action known as the Anschluss (unification), Adolf Hitler declares Austria to be part of Germany and enforces the declaration with German troops in Austria.

July 6–14—Evian Conference discusses plight of Jews in Nazi-held countries.

September 28–29—At Munich Conference, England and France allow Germany to take over the western area of Czechoslovakia known as the Sudetenland.

October 1—Germany annexes the Sudetenland.

November 9–10—Nazi violence against Jews on Kristallnacht stirs sympathy in England toward Jews.

November 16—British Parliament debates idea of giving refuge to Jews in Nazi territories.

December—British government gives official authorization for Kindertransports.

December 1—First Kindertransport leaves Berlin with 196 children from a Jewish orphanage; it arrives in Harwich on December 2.

December 8—Lord Baldwin makes public appeal for funds for Jewish refugees.

December 10—Second Kindertransport, the first from Vienna, leaves; it reaches Harwich on December 11.

1939

March 14—First Kindertransport train from Prague leaves.

March 15—Germany invades and occupies most of Czechoslovakia.

September 1—Germany invades Poland, beginning World War II; Kindertransport due to leave Prague does not leave.

November—British government orders all citizens of enemy countries ages sixteen and older to register as enemy aliens.

1940

May 14—The Netherlands surrenders to Germany; last Kindertransport leaves the Netherlands.

May and June—British government places enemy aliens in internment camps.

July 2—*Arandora Star* is torpedoed and sunk as it is taking enemy aliens to Canada.

July 10–September 6—*Dunera* sails from Liverpool to Sydney, Australia, with 2,500 internees.

1989

June—More than 1,200 Kinder are reunited in England.

Introduction. Number 152

1. Lore Groszmann Segal, *Other People's Houses* (New York: Harcourt, Brace, and World, 1958, 1961, 1962, 1964), pp. 22–23.
2. Ibid., p. 30.
3. Lore Groszmann's story from her autobiography: Lore Groszmann Segal, *Other People's Houses* (New York: Harcourt, Brace, and World, 1958, 1961, 1962, 1964).

Chapter 1. The German Idealist: Norbert Wollheim

1. Norbert Wollheim, Interview, United States Holocaust Memorial Museum (USHMM), October 5 and October 17, 1990, <http://www.wollheim-memorial.de/en/lebensgeschichtliche_interviews> (November 10, 2009).
2. Wollheim, cited in Mark Jonathan Harris and Deborah Oppenheimer, *Into the Arms of Strangers: Stories of the Kindertransport* (New York: MJF Books, 2000), p. 32.
3. Wollheim, First Interview, USHMM, October 5, 1991, Transcript, p. 18, <http://www.wollheim-memorial.de/en/juedische_jugendbewegung_en> (January 18, 2009).
4. Wollheim, Interview, USHMM, October 5 and October 17, 1990, <http://www.wollheim-memorial.de/en/lebensgeschichtliche_interviews> (November 10, 2009).
5. Ibid.
6. Wollheim, First Interview, USHMM, October 5, 1991, Transcript, pp. 44–45, <http://www.wollheim-memorial.de/en/norbert_wollheims_beteiligung_an_der_organisation_der_Kindertransporte> (January 18, 2009).
7. Wollheim, Interview, USHMM, 1992, <http://www.ushmm.org/wlc/media_oi.php?lang=en&ModuleId=10005260&MediaId=2489> (January 18, 2009).

8. Wollheim, First Interview, USHMM, October 5, 1991, Transcript, p. 49, <http://www.wollheim-memorial.de/en/juedische_jugendbewegung_en> (January 18, 2009).

9. Wollheim, Interview, USHMM, 1992, <http://www.ushmm.org/outreach/en/media_oi.php?MediaId=1190> (November 10, 2009).

Chapter 2. The Dutch Aunt: Gertrud Wijsmuller-Meijer

1. Cited by Paul Kohn, "I Was Among the Lucky Ones," *Haartz*, December 11, 2008.

2. Lord Baldwin, radio broadcast, of December 8, 1938, widely reported in the British newspapers on the following day. *The Times*, December 9, 1938.

3. Gertrud Wijsmuller-Meijer, testimony at Yad Vashem, 1961, cited by Aaron Schart in article for University of Duiseberg-Essen, 2001, <http://translate. google.com/translate?hl=en&sl=de&u=http://www.uni-duisburg-essen.de/ Ev-Theologie/courses/course-stuff/kinderD5.htm&sa=X&oi=translate&resn um=9&ct=result&prev=/search%3Fq%3DEichmann%2BWijsmuller%26sta rt%3D10%26hl%3Den%26rls%3DDMUS,DMUS:2006- 32,DMUS:en%26sa%3DN> (January 15, 2009).

4. Lore Groszmann Segal, *Other People's Houses* (New York: Harcourt, Brace, and World, 1958, 1961, 1962, 1964), pp. 32–33.

5. Story told by Norbert Wollheim, Interview, United States Holocaust Memorial Museum, October 5, 1991, Transcript, pp. 41–43, <http:// www.wollheim-memorial.de/en/norbert_wollheims_beteiligung_an_der_ organisation_der_Kindertransporte> (January 18, 2009).

6. Manfred Alweiss, "My Exodus From Berlin," *Kindertransport Newsletter*, April 2006, <http://www.ajr.org.uk/documents/ktapr06.pdf> (April 17, 2008).

7. From Lo Vrooland, *Geen tijd voor tranen* [*No Time for Tears: The Wartime Memories of Truus Wijsmuller*] (Amsterdam: Van Kampen, 1961). Interview with Geertruida (Truus) Wijsmuller-Meijer, 1951, Netherlands Institute for War Documentation NIOD, Amsterdam, Archive Geertruida Wijsmuller- Meijer. Cited in Daphne L. Meijer, "Unknown Children: The Last Train from Westerbork," in *Children and the Holocaust: Symposium Presentations* (Washington, DC: United States Holocaust Memorial Museum Center for Advanced Holocaust Studies, 2004), pp. 98–99. Available online: <http:// www.ushmm.org/research/center/publications/occasional/2004-09/paper .pdf> (January 20, 2009).

Chapter 3. **The British Stockbroker: Nicholas Winton**

1. Nicholas Winton, cited in *Nicholas Winton: The Power of Good*, Gelman Educational Foundation, 2008, <http://www.powerofgood.net/story.php> (January 5, 2009).
2. Nicholas Winton, radio interview with David Vaughan, Radio Praha, transcript in *Cesky Rozhlas* magazine, June 19, 2002, <http://www.radio.cz/en/article/30418> (November 25, 2009).
3. Ibid.
4. Ibid.
5. Winton, cited in *Nicholas Winton: The Power of Good*.
6. "Nicholas Winton and the Rescue of Children from Czechoslovakia, 1938–1939," *Holocaust Encyclopedia*, n.d., <http://www.ushmm.org/wlc/article.php?lang=en&ModuleId=10007780> (January 13, 2009).
7. Winton, cited in *Nicholas Winton: The Power of Good*.
8. Vera Gissing, cited by Patrick Barkham, "Nicholas Winton, Secret Hero Who Saved Jewish Children From the Nazis Is Lauded, 50 Years On," *Times Online*, 2002, <http://www.raoulwallenberg.net/?en/press/nicholas-winton-secret-hero.5011018.htm> (December 3, 2009).

Chapter 4. **A Family in England: Kurt Fuchel**

1. Kurt Fuchel, "Vienna, 1938: A Child's View," Voices of the Kinder, *Kindertransport Association* (KTA), n.d., <http://www.kindertransport.org/memoirs/memoir-fuchel-02.html> (January 14, 2009).
2. Ibid.
3. Ibid.
4. Kurt Fuchel, cited in Mark Jonathan Harris and Deborah Oppenheimer, *Into the Arms of Strangers: Stories of the Kindertransport* (New York: MJF Books, 2000), p. 126.
5. Ibid., pp. 201–202.
6. Ibid., pp. 233–234.

Chapter 5. **A Bittersweet Rescue: Bertha Engelhard Leverton**

1. Bertha Engelhard Leverton, "Migration in Golders Green: Bertha Leverton's Story," *London Grid for Learning*, n.d., <http://www.lgfl.net/lgfl/leas/barnet/

accounts/migration/web/other_stories/media/What%20the%20journey%20 to%20England%20was%20like.doc> (January 19, 2009).

2. Bertha Leverton, cited in Mark Jonathan Harris and Deborah Oppenheimer, *Into the Arms of Strangers: Stories of the Kindertransport* (New York: MJF Books, 2000), p. 88.

3. Leverton, "Migration in Golders Green."

4. Ibid.

5. Leverton, cited in Harris and Oppenheimer, p. 147.

6. Ibid., pp. 209–210.

7. Coventry Blitz Remembered: Letters, *Coventry Evening Telegraph*, November 12, 2004.

8. Leverton, "Migration in Golders Green."

Chapter 6. New Brothers and Sisters: The Attenborough Family

1. Cited in Richard Brooks, "The Attenborough Sisters Who Escaped Hitler," *Sunday Times*, November 30, 2008, <http://www.timesonline.co.uk/tol/news/ uk/article5257601.ece> (January 29, 2009).

2. Richard Attenborough, interviewed by Nigel Farndale in "Richard Attenborough: The Trouper," *Telegraph*, December 23, 2007, <http://www .telegraph.co.uk/culture/3670132/Richard-Attenborough-the-trouper.html> (December 9, 2009).

3. Cited by Richard Attenborough in "Triumph of the Spirit: Richard Attenborough Interview," by Catherine Deveney in *Scotland on Sunday*, September 14, 2008, <http://scotlandonsunday.scotsman.com/spectrum/ Triumph-of-the-spirit-.4487306.jp> (December 9, 2009).

4. Richard Brooks.

5. Richard Attenborough, Preface to *Into the Arms of Strangers: Stories of the Kindertransport* by Mark Jonathan Harris and Deborah Oppenheimer (New York: MJF Books, 2000), p. x.

6. Ibid.

Chapter 7. Enemy Alien: Walter Kohn

1. Walter Kohn, "Walter Kohn: The Nobel Prize in Chemistry 1998, Autobiography," *Nobelprize.org*, 1998, <http://nobelprize.org/nobel_prizes/ chemistry/laureates/1998/kohn-autobio.html> (November 18, 2008).

2. Cited by Norman Rose, *Churchill: The Unruly Giant* (New York: Simon and Schuster, 1994), p. 326.

3. Rabbi Solomon Schonfeld, *A Report on Visits to Internment Camps for Aliens (July 16-23, 1940)*, 2009, <http://www.jewishvirtuallibrary.org/jsource/Holocaust/chiefrabbi.html> (January 18, 2009).

4. Ibid.

5. Ibid.

6. Winston Churchill, *The Second World War* (Boston: Houghton Mifflin Harcourt, 1985), p. 529.

7. Walter Kohn.

8. Ibid.

9. Walter Kohn, cited by Sarah Healey in *Holocaust Survivors and Remembrance Project: "Forget You Not,"* January 17, 2001, <http://isurvived.org/Kohn_Walter-HolocaustNobel.html> (December 11, 2009).

Chapter 8. On the Hell Ship: Abrascha Gorbulski

1. Alexander Gordon (Abrascha Gorbulski), cited in Mark Jonathan Harris and Deborah Oppenheimer, *Into the Arms of Strangers: Stories of the Kindertransport* (New York: MJF Books, 2000), p. 45.

2. Ibid., p. 223.

3. Ibid., p. 140.

4. Unnamed Kind, cited by Bethan James in "Welsh Haven for Jewish Children," *BBC Wales*, January 26, 2006, <http://news.bbc.co.uk/2/hi/uk_news/wales/north_east/4648406.stm> (December 18, 2009).

5. *Dunera Memorandum*, cited in "Activity 14: Seeking Asylum: A Case Study," *Holocaust Educational Trust*, n.d., <http://www.thinkequal.com/page.cfm/link=169> (December 13, 2009).

6. Walter Kaufmann, cited by Kate Connolly in "Britons Finally Learn the Dark Dunera Secret," *Sydney Morning Herald*, 2006, <http://www.smh.com.au/news/film/britons-finally-learn-the-dark-dunera-secret/2006/05/18/1147545457055.html> (January 20, 2009).

7. Gordon, cited in Harris and Oppenheimer, p. 189.

Chapter 9. Two Cousins, Two Stories: Madeleine Albright and Dagmar Simova

1. Her father's name was Josef Korböl; in the Czech language, names of females have "ova" added to the end.
2. Cited in Michael Dobbs, *Madeleine Albright: A Twentieth Century Odyssey* (New York: Henry Holt, 1999), p. 43.
3. Cited in "Secretary of State Discovers Jewish Roots," *Jewish News of Greater Phoenix*, vol. 49, no. 21, February 7, 1997, <http://www.jewishaz.com/jewishnews/970207/secstate.html> (January 16, 2009).
4. Cited by Michael Dobbs in "Out of the Past," *Washington Post*, February 9, 1997, <http://www.washingtonpost.com/wp-srv/politics/govt/admin/stories/albright020997.htm> (January 14, 2009).
5. "Secretary of State Discovers Jewish Roots."
6. Michael Dobbs, "Out of the Past."
7. Ibid.

Afterword

1. Holocaust Kindertransport, n.d., <http://www.holocaustkinder.com/> (December 3, 2009).
2. Mark Jonathan Harris and Deborah Oppenheimer, *Into the Arms of Strangers: Stories of the Kindertransport* (New York: MJF Books, 2000), pp. 250–251.
3. Bertha Engelhard Leverton, "Migration in Golders Green: Bertha Leverton's Story," *London Grid for Learning*, n.d., <http://www.lgfl.net/lgfl/leas/barnet/accounts/migration/web/other_stories/media/What%20life%20in%20%20England%20was%20like%20for%20her%20as%20a%20transportee.doc> (January 19, 2009).
4. Kurt Fuchel, "Vienna, 1938: A Child's View," Voices of the Kinder, *Kindertransport Association* (KTA), n.d., <http://www.kindertransport.org/memoirs/memoir-fuchel-02.html> (January 14, 2009).
5. Charlotte Levy, in Harris and Oppenheimer, p. 253.
6. Nicholas Winton, cited in Lawrence W. Reed and Benjamin D. Stafford, "The Difference One Can Make," *Mackinac Center for Public Policy*, August 17, 2006, <http://www.mackinac.org/article.aspx?ID=7872> (January 29, 2009).

Anschluss (German for "unification")—The action whereby Austria became part of Germany by Hitler's declaration and military force.

"Aryan"—A term misused by Nazis to refer to a person of pure-blooded Germanic background, typically tall, blonde, and blue-eyed.

asylum—A place where a person is protected from arrest.

blitzkrieg—Literally "lightning war," name for German military tactic of attacking quickly and without warning.

Gentile—A non-Jewish person.

Gestapo—The *Geheime Staatspolizei*, the State Secret Police of Nazi Germany.

Hanukkah—Also known as the Festival of Lights, an eight-day Jewish holiday commemorating the rededication of the Holy Temple in Jerusalem at the time of the Maccabean revolt. It usually falls between late November and late December.

hostel—Supervised short-term housing.

intern—Confine; internment usually refers to confining, or imprisoning, people who are not guilty of a crime but are considered security risks.

Kind (plural Kinder)—German word for "child."

Mischling—Literally "mixture," term used for a person with one Jewish and one non-Jewish parent.

Nazi—Member of, or pertaining to, the National Socialist German Worker's Party, a political organization founded on the principles of extreme nationalism, militarism, racism, and one-party control.

orthodox—Following accepted rules. An Orthodox Jew is one who adheres strictly to traditional beliefs and practices of Judaism.

Parliament—In England, group that makes laws.

rucksack—British word for backpack.

sanctuary—A safe place.

SS (*Schutzstaffel*)—Literally "protection squad," a huge military-like organization that provided guards and policing units to the Nazis.

synagogue—Jewish house of worship.

tram—British word for streetcar.

visa—A document issued by a government that gives a person permission to leave or enter a country. Countries issue exit visas, transit visas (permitting people to pass through), and various types of entry visas.

Fox, Anne L., and Eva Abraham-Podietz. *Ten Thousand Children: True Stories Told by Children Who Escaped the Holocaust on the Kindertransport*. Springfield, N.J.: Behrman House, 1998.

Golabek, Mona, and Lee Cohen. *The Children of Willesden Lane: Beyond the Kindertransport: A Memoir of Music, Love, and Survival*. New York: Warner Books, 2003.

Goldstein, Susy, Gina Hamilton, and Wendy Share. *Ten Marks and a Train Ticket: Benno's Escape to Freedom*. Toronto: League for Human Rights of B'nai Brith Canada, 2008.

Harris, Mark Jonathan, and Deborah Oppenheimer. *Into the Arms of Strangers: Stories of the Kindertransport*. New York: MJF, 2000.

Korobkin, Frieda. *Throw Your Feet Over Your Shoulders: Beyond the Kindertransport*. Manchester, U.K.: Devora, 2008.

Turner, Barry. *One Small Suitcase*. London: Puffin, 2003.

Zullo, Allan, and Mara Bovsun. *Survivors: True Stories of Children in the Holocaust*. New York: Scholastic, 2004.

Association of Jewish Refugees (AJR): Kindertransport
   <http://www.ajr.org.uk/kindertransport>

The Kindertransport Association (KTA)
   <http://www.kindertransport.org/>

United States Holocaust Memorial Museum

Levy, Charlotte, 111

M
Mauthausen, 29
Mendel, Bruno, 88–89
Mischlings, 74

N
Nazi brutality. *See also* Germany.
    antisemitic laws, 7–8, 14–18,
        51–52, 60, 69, 80
    bombing raids, 70
    deportations, 17, 23–25, 29,
        38, 74, 77, 91–92
    disappearing people, 46
    forced labor, 24–25, 29, 77
    harassment, 35–36, 45
    theft, 22, 33
the Netherlands, 29, 32–39, 64, 83
Nuremberg laws, 17

P
Palestine, 37, 90–91, 94
Poland, 17, 37, 45, 75, 82, 92
psychological effects, 56, 76, 110–
    111

R
refugee camps, 40–41, 65–67
Refugee Children's Movement,
    26–28
Reunion of Kinder, 72
reunion with parents, family, 13,
    20, 58–59
Righteous Gentiles, 39

S
Saden, Inge Engelhard, 62, 63, 68,
    70, 71, 110

Schonfeld, Solomon, 84–85, 94
Simova, Dagmar, 101–109
sponsors, 16, 26–27, 43–45, 65–68,
    80, 93
Sudetenland region, 40, 41
Sweden, 23, 37, 42, 43, 86

T
Theresienstadt, 77
training farms, 81–82, 91, 94
transit camps, 29, 38–39
Treaty of Versailles, 86

U
U-boats, 86, 87
United States
    emigration to, 25, 59, 77, 89,
        100, 107
    issues in reaching, 73, 75, 95,
        103
    refusal of children by, 42

W
Westerbork, 38–39
Wijsmuller-Meyer, Gertrud, 28–39
Winton, Grete, 47
Winton, Nicholas, 40–49, 103, 113
Wollheim, Norbert, 14–25

Y
Yad Vashem, 39
Youth Aliyah, 94
youth hostels, 93–95
Yugoslavia, 101, 103, 105, 109